Precious Stones & Alabaster

Gifts of Advice for Christian Women Starting College

Lori Barstow White

Precious Stones & Alabaster

SECOND EDITION

Interior: Ellen C. Maze, The Author's Mentor, www.ellencmaze.com
Author Photo Credit: Billy Sanford

ISBN-13: 978-1475048094
Also available in eBook

PRINTED IN THE UNITED STATES OF AMERICA

The words of King David:

Now with all my ability I have provided for the house of my God the gold for the things of gold, and the silver for the things of silver, and the bronze for the things of bronze, the iron for the things of iron, and wood for the things of wood, onyx stones and inlaid stones, stones of antimony and stones of various colors, *and all kinds of precious stones and alabaster in abundance.*

1 Chronicles 29:2 (NASB)

This book is dedicated
to my very own jewels...

In memory
Ruby Jeannette Harris Floyd
Leonora Douglas Barstow

In gratitude
Sammie Jo Floyd Barstow
Leslie Rae Barstow Sulenski

In hope
Danielle Elise Sulenski
Mavinee Ann White

How to use *Precious Stones & Alabaster* for your first semester in college...

You probably have a lot of questions and concerns about your first semester of college. It's my hope to communicate with students on a practical and spiritual level regarding many of the experiences awaiting you. It's my prayer that these gifts of advice will provide you with at least some of the practical information and spiritual guidance you will need.

This devotional book is divided into twelve weeks with five days of reading each week. After each daily reading, you'll have the opportunity to journal about the day's topic. I hope you'll take time each day to record your thoughts. These journal entries will not only be a great opportunity for you to express your thoughts about your college experience, but you'll enjoy reading back over them later. I'm sure you'll be amazed at your own personal and spiritual growth during the semester.

The weekly topics are designed to follow you through the semester. As your college experience grows, the weekly topics will expand with you. Some things about college can only be fully understood as they are experienced, so if you choose to read ahead, go back and check out the information in a given week as you come to that week during the semester.

At the end of each day, you'll find a practical piece of advice called *Rubies*. These rubies are suggestions you can implement immediately. I've picked up many "rubies" of advice from my own students, and I'm happy to pass them along to you.

I hope your first semester in college is a wonderful experience. I'm praying for you!

~ Lori Barstow White

Table of Contents

First Week

Welcome to the World, Baby Girl!

There are worlds in an Opal.

- Astrid Alauda

Week 1, Day 1

Treasures of Wisdom and Knowledge

Congratulations! As you start your first semester of college, you deserve a round of applause. You might believe all your high school classmates are thinking about or planning to go to college. Maybe you have parents or other family members who have always expected you to go to college, so it doesn't seem like anything out of the ordinary. Why the congratulations?

Believe it or not, only 1% of the world's population has a college degree. That's amazing isn't it? From the perspective of the entire world, higher education is a possibility for very few people. Even in America, the idea of attending college seems out of reach for many people because of financial constraints, family obligations or the fear of failing to succeed academically. If you are dealing with any of these hurdles and you're still attending college, another round of applause, please!

I believe my college education is a tremendous gift from God. I think higher education is a noble pursuit and will serve you for a lifetime. Your education is one of the few things you have that cannot be lost or taken. We know as Christians that God has a plan for our lives. According to Acts 17, He has planned where we will live and in what time we will live, so seek His guidance constantly through the process of making your plans for college.

As an academic advisor, I want to use these daily thoughts to help you make a successful transition from high school to college. I will share information I've learned, not only as a professional in higher education, but also what I learned as a new college student myself. Some of those lessons are timeless and are still applicable to today's college student. Others have changed, and I continue to gain new insights from my students as they learn to adapt to college life. My students are a constant source of new education for me, and I know their experiences will serve as great examples for you this semester.

As a Christian, I want to use this information to encourage and prepare you for what God has planned for your life as a college student. College is a place where you will learn how to learn. But whether you major in theatre, biology, business or psychology, the greatest lesson learned is found in Colossians 2:2-3 (NIV).

My purpose is that they may be
encouraged in heart and united in love,
so that they may have the full riches of
complete understanding, in order that
they may know the mystery of God,
namely, Christ, in whom are hidden all
the treasures of wisdom and knowledge.

Education, wisdom and knowledge are purposeless without Christ. It is my prayer that as you increase in knowledge through education that your understanding of and relationship with the Savior will increase also. This is going to be a great adventure. Let's get started!

- What challenges to attending college do you face as you start this first semester?

- Who has given you the most encouragement as you have planned to start college?

My purpose is that they may be encouraged in heart and united in love, so that they may have the full riches of complete understanding, in order that they may know the mystery of God, namely, Christ, in whom are hidden all the treasures of wisdom and knowledge.
Col. 2:2-3 (NIV)

Rubies:

Make sure to locate your classrooms before you go to class for the first time. Take a copy of your schedule and walk around campus to each of the buildings. You don't want to get lost and end up late for class the first day!

Week 1, Day 2

Do Not Fear

I don't have much trouble remembering how I felt as I started my first week of college. It's likely that some of those emotions have been forgotten over time, but I know one I felt for sure: sheer terror! There were so many new people, a brand new place and so many classrooms. How in the world do you find the right classroom in a place this big? I'm certain the administration tries to frustrate the students by numbering classrooms with odd numbers on one hall and even numbers on the other, or by giving them a number like 1430-C. It can be so confusing!

Walking into a college classroom for the first time is daunting. I started college with several good friends, but inevitably we would have separate classes, and I would have to go into a new classroom where there were no familiar faces. I never knew where to sit – maybe someone was holding a seat for a friend. I can remember distinctly the feeling of wanting to get in a seat and just be invisible. Hopefully, the professor would not call on me, and I prayed fervently that we wouldn't have to go around the room and introduce ourselves.

Every student has a different set of worries. Some want to make a good impression on new people. Others are concerned about the logistics of finding their way around campus. Moving from a quiet suburban home with one sibling to a huge residence hall can also be cause for anxiety.

If these are some of your fears as you start your first week of college, it's probable that all your fellow new students are feeling the same things. I can't tell you how many students have leaned into my desk and said in a low voice, "Is everybody as scared as I am?" Yes, they are. I'm sure you'll see other students and think they look confident and secure. Don't be fooled! Inside they are worried about the same things you are – getting to the right place on time, making new friends, and doing the laundry without turning everything pink.

The best news is that God is with you and does not want you to be afraid.

Do not fear, for I am with you; Do not anxiously look about you, for I am your God. I will strengthen you, surely I will help you, surely I will uphold you with My righteous right hand. ~ Isaiah 41:10 (NASB)

Do you know how many times the words "Do not fear" appear in the Bible? In the Old Testament, God asks his followers not to fear literally dozens of times. Jesus issues the same command in the New Testament eight times to disciples or followers. We are truly encouraged to have a spirit of hope and not of fear.

Call on God this week as you confront fears about starting college and being in a new place. He is with you and will surely uphold you.

- What fears do you have as you start college? Write them as a prayer here and ask God to deliver you from them:

Do not fear, for I am with you; Do not anxiously look about you, for I am your God. I will strengthen you, surely will I help you, surely I will uphold you with My righteous right hand. Isaiah 41:10 (NASB)

Rubies:

When you go into an unfamiliar classroom for the first time, find someone sitting alone and sit next to them. Speak first – you never know where you might find a new friend.

Week 1, Day 3

Don't Look for Shortcuts!

My students tell me the hardest part about starting college is getting used to how extremely different it is from the typical high school experience. In high school, someone else structures your day. In college, you choose your schedule. In high school, you have only a few choices about the courses you take during the year. In college, you can select courses from what is usually an enormous list. Essentially, most students change from having an extremely structured school day to one only as structured as they choose to make it. This can be overwhelming for a new college student.

It can also be exciting! You finally have some say in how you spend your time and what subjects you will study. Most students have the option to choose elective courses that are fun: aerobics classes, sewing or cooking classes or even classes on how to change the oil in your car. Recently, my university offered a course titled *The Boys of Summer* about the history of baseball. These kinds of classes can be lots of fun and a diversion from the hum-drum of more academic courses. But remember, these courses need to be a fun addition to your schedule, not your entire schedule!

During summer orientation, I am constantly talking with new students who want to fill up their first semester with electives and put off taking their required courses. A semester of golf, swimming, and photography sounds like a lot of fun, but a schedule full of electives not only postpones achieving your goal of finishing a degree, it makes subsequent semesters much more difficult because you don't have those fun classes to add when you need them.

Avoid taking shortcuts with your schedule the first year. Go ahead and dive on in with some solid classes that are required for your chosen major. Sign up for those math and history classes – or any of the subjects you might be wary of. Trust me, later you will be glad you took the recommended classes, and you'll be able to see that you've made real progress toward your degree.

Matthew 7:13-14 has great advice for believers seeking success not only in life but in their relationship with God:

> *Don't look for shortcuts to God. The market is flooded with surefire, easygoing formulas for a successful life that can be practiced in your spare time. Don't fall for that stuff, even though crowds of people do. The way to life – to God! – is vigorous and requires total attention. (MSG)*

Give "vigorous attention" to everything in which you desire success, whether it is in pursuit of God or in scheduling college classes. Try to picture your senior year. Your schedule will likely include 400-level courses with huge demands on your time and energy. You'll need some elective classes to buffer against all the work that will come with a senior-level course load. Use your freedom to select courses wisely, and take the advice of the university advisors who are there to help you make a schedule for success.

- Look through your college catalog and pick out classes that you think would be fun to take with your schedule in future semesters. List them here:

- When scheduling courses for this current semester, did you receive any good advice from someone who worked in your college? Write it here so you can remember it for later.

Rubies:

Look for "Freshman Seminar" or "Orientation to College" classes to take for an elective during your first or second semester. Most colleges offer them, and these classes are great sources of information about the college and campus life.

Don't look for shortcuts to God. The market is flooded with surefire, easygoing formulas for a successful life that can be practiced in your spare time. Don't fall for that stuff, even though crowds of people do. The way to life – to God! – is vigorous and requires total attention. Matt 7:13-14 (MSG)

Week 1, Day 4

Open-Minded Wisdom

Spring Break this year was a grand, international adventure. I had the rare privilege to travel to Santa Clara, Brazil with three students from my university on a cultural exchange and mission trip. Christie, Kelli, Kelly and I met frequently during the months before our trip, planned out as many details as possible and shared our enthusiasm over the upcoming journey. One of the most exciting parts for me was that this would be Christie and Kelly's first trip out of the country. I prayed so hard for them. I wanted them to have a great experience, an adventure they would remember for the rest of their lives.

Traveling to another country requires flexibility and a spirit of adaptability. Anything can happen! The girls and I traveled 28 hours to reach our destination in Brazil, utilizing two planes, two buses, and one van packed with our luggage. Combine that with the blazing heat, lack of air conditioning, and very little sleep, and you'd think complaints would abound. Not with these students. They had planned ahead to have an open mind and to lean into the challenges.

I noticed early that Kelly was definitely up for the full experience of traveling to Brazil. She wanted to try every new fruit, juice or dessert that came her way. She explored every new place, ran full-speed down the beach, hugged every child, and even learned praise songs in Portuguese. Kelly had a fabulous attitude and was determined to try out everything new. Did she find anything about Brazil she didn't like? Nope, she loved it all. Kelly's open-minded attitude certainly made the difference in her experience. Solomon would call her wise.

Cynics look high and low for wisdom –
and never find it; the open-minded find it
right on their doorstep!
Proverbs 14:6 (MSG)

Kelly's approach to Brazil is a great example to follow as you start college. I'm sure your college campus must seem like a foreign country to you. Everyone is speaking a different language, the scenery and food are different and there are so many people you haven't met. It would be easy to hang back and stay uninvolved, but you would miss the adventure.

Get out there and try new things! One great way to make new friends is to be the first to introduce yourself to your neighbors. Everyone is hesitant about meeting new people. Break the ice first and invite someone to lunch. Speaking of food, try a new on-campus restaurant at least once a week. Some of the best campus cuisine might be right around the corner. I'm sure your college has great on-campus events each semester, also. Go see a play, a movie, or a concert.

Your attitude can help or hinder your experience in the first few weeks of college. Think like Kelly and decide that you are going to get the best out of each new experience. Be bold in your exploration, stepping out of your comfort zone. I hope you love the first few weeks on campus as much as Kelly loved Brazil. And the best part is that you will probably have air conditioning!

- Be honest – in what ways are you closed minded about starting college? What negative, preconceived notions did you bring from home?

- What can you do this week to step out and try something new? Pick an event on campus and commit below to attend:

Cynics look high and low for wisdom – and never find it; the open-minded find it right on their doorstep! Proverbs 14:6 (MSG)

Rubies:

Seek out friends who have an obvious zest for experiencing all the great aspects of college life. Surrounding yourself with people who are positive and adventurous will help you become more open-minded.

Week 1, Day 5

Freedom

Kris Kristofferson wrote a song in the late 1960s that has been recorded and re-recorded for decades. *Me and Bobby McGee* was made famous by Janis Joplin in 1971, but she wasn't the first to record it. More recently, country music artist LeAnn Rimes put her own spin on this classic. Even if every lyric is not committed to memory, you're probably familiar with the famous line from the chorus: *Freedom's just another word for nothing left to lose.* The song is about two kids hitchhiking across the country with no responsibilities weighing them down. It's a romantic idea, which is probably why the song has been so popular.

I would assume you have more freedom right now than you have ever experienced. You may have had strict rules growing up, or very few, but living on your own is completely different from the family life you've experienced up to now. For the first time in your life, there's not someone around to wake you up, sit with you when you're sick, remind you about a club meeting or help with the laundry. All responsibility falls to you, and it can be overwhelming.

Are you ready for the challenge of being on your own? Unfortunately, this kind of freedom comes with a lot to lose. Bobby McGee might have all the freedom in the world, but yours comes with a lot of responsibility. Misuse this freedom and you can do some significant damage.

But freedom can be a wonderful thing, too. You are able to make your own decisions about how and with whom you spend your time, what types of activities you want to participate in and even how late you sleep. It's prime time to find out what works for you, what doesn't, and how to adapt to new situations.

Read this passage from Romans about freedom in God:

Since we're free in the freedom of God, can we do anything that comes to mind? Hardly. You know well enough from your own experience that there are some acts of so-called freedom that destroy freedom. Offer yourselves to sin, for instance, and it's your last free act. But offer yourselves to the ways of God and the freedom never quits.
Romans 6:15 (MSG)

As a Christian you have ample freedom in God through your faith. But Paul warns his readers that even in this most blessed freedom, there are "acts of so-called freedom" that will destroy it. Take Paul's message here and apply it to the freedom you are experiencing this semester. For example, you are free to sleep as late as you wish, but if you miss class you'll be unprepared for the next test. In the same way, you're free to party every night of the week, but ultimately your college performance will suffer.

Prove yourself worthy of this new freedom. Don't misuse it like a hitchhiker traveling across country. Treat it as a precious gift given to make you stronger, more responsible, and trustworthy.

- In what ways are you most looking forward to having the kind of freedom that comes with college life?

- What advice have you been given by others about managing your freedom and being responsible?

- Ask God to help you be responsible with your freedom.

Since we're free in the freedom of God, can we do anything that comes to mind? Hardly. You know well enough from your own experience that there are some acts of so-called freedom that destroy freedom. Offer yourselves to sin, for instance, and it's your last free act. But offer yourselves to the ways of God and the freedom never quits. Romans 6:15 (MSG)

Rubies:

The best advice regarding freedom might be to go slowly. Don't plunge in head first and try out all your new freedoms at once, take it slow and enjoy the process. Moderation may pay off in the end because all freedom comes with responsibility.

My Notes:

Second Week

The Language of College

The questions are diamonds you hold in the light. Study a lifetime and you see different colors from the same jewel. The same questions, asked again, bring you just the answers you need just the minute you need them.

- Richard Bach

Week 2, Day 1

The Language of College

While visiting Guinea, West Africa several years ago, I was so excited to attend my first bilingual church service. I just assumed one of the languages would be English. But, to my surprise, the service was conducted entirely in French and an African heart-language, Susu. I don't speak either of those languages! I could certainly comprehend the passion of the two speakers, but I missed all the content.

The language of college can sound foreign to new students, but it's a language you need to learn in order to navigate the system. Paul wrote, "There are many languages in the world and they all mean something to someone." (I Corinthians 14:10, MSG). Listed below are common terms used in the college language. Make sure you are familiar with these because they are important to your success as a student.

- **Audit**: Students can "audit" a course by attending and participating in the class without receiving credit. Permission from the instructor is usually required.

- **Bachelor's Degree:** The undergraduate degree offered by four-year colleges and universities. This degree usually requires a minimum of 120 credit hours.
- **Credit Hours:** College courses are measured in credit hours. A course worth 1 credit hour usually meets for one class period per week. Most courses are 3 credit hours and meet three hours per week. Typically, courses are offered for 1-5 credit hours.
- **Catalog:** The catalog provides vital information concerning your degree program and requirements, contact information, scholarships, financial aid, student life activities and core requirements. Having a copy or knowing where to find it online is a must.
- **Concurrent Enrollment**: Some universities will let students enroll in courses at more than one institution. For example, some of my students take courses at the local community college while they are enrolled at the university.
- **Curriculum:** A curriculum is the list of courses required to complete a degree program of study.
- **Drop/Add:** Students are given the opportunity to change the content of their schedules for a few days at the first of a semester. Permission from an instructor and/or a fee may be required.
- **FAFSA:** Free Application for Federal Student Aid, the application used at almost every institution. A completed FAFSA is required for some scholarship applications and for all financial aid awards.

As you can see, there are many new words and phrases to learn in college. Take the time to make learning these terms a priority. Let's talk about this more tomorrow. For now check out the journaling assignment for today. Do any of these words look like they are part of a foreign language?

Find your college catalog and define the following terms according to your institution:

- Concurrent Enrollment: Is it approved for your college?
- What is required to "audit" a course?
- What is the last day you can drop a course this semester?
- Where can you find a list of courses required for your curriculum?
- How many credit hours are required to be a full-time student at your college?

There are many languages in the world and they all mean something to someone.
I Cor 14:10 (MSG)

Rubies:

College catalogs are usually available on-line. If you have trouble finding a term, you can always use a search engine. At least that way you don't have to remember where you put your catalog!

Week 2, Day 2

More Lessons on Language

Paul encouraged believers in Corinth to make sure their church services were understood by everyone in order to effectively spread the gospel. Evidently, some believers were speaking in private prayer languages known only to them and God. Paul said this was great for the believer, but it wasn't edifying to others who couldn't understand.

If you give a blessing using your private prayer language, which no one else understands, how can some outsider who has just shown up and has no idea what's going on know when to say, "Amen"? Your blessing might be beautiful, but you have very effectively cut that person out of it.
1Corinthians 14:16-17 (MSG)

I don't want you to feel like you are the outsider who has just shown up for college and doesn't have any idea what's going on! Let's go over some more terms used in the language of college so you'll be up to speed.

- **GPA:** Grade Point Average. Colleges use both letter grades and GPAs. Points are assigned to letter grades as follows: A=4, B=3, C=2, D=1, F=0 per credit hour. Simply take the points assigned to the letter grade, multiply it by the credit hours and divide by the credit hours to get the GPA for the courses. Example: A student makes an "A" in a 3-hour Biology class and a "C" in a 3-hour English class. The "A" is worth 12 points; the "C" is worth 6 points. Those points divided by 6 (for the hours of credit) will give the student a 3.0 GPA.

- **Academic Suspension:** If a student fails to maintain the minimum required GPA established by the college, suspension can result. A student placed on suspension will be dismissed from the college for at least one semester.
- **Pass/Fail Courses:** These classes are not assigned letter grades on the transcript. A "Pass" in these courses is assigned if the minimum standards were met. The student will receive credit hours but not GPA points. Many schools will factor a "Fail" into the GPA, so find out that information ahead of time!
- **Prerequisite:** A course that is required before another can be taken. For example, English 101 is usually a prerequisite for English 102.
- **Syllabus:** A detailed description of a course and the requirements for completing it. You should receive a syllabus for every class with information on how to contact the professor and what to do if you need special accommodations.

We're running out of room, so take a little more time with your catalog and today's journaling assignment. Do you feel like you're learning more about the language of college? I hope so!

Use your catalog to look up the following terms and how they are defined by your college:

- **Withdrawal:** What are the requirements for a semester or a class?
- **Transcript:** Where can you get a copy?
- **Registrar:** Who is this person in your college and what does he/she do?
- **Schedule of Classes:** Where can you get a copy?
- **Mid-term Exams:** Do any of your classes have them?
- **Probation:** What are the penalties? Is it different from suspension?

Rubies:

Calculating your GPA can be difficult to learn. Many schools have GPA calculators on the main website. Those are great! Just plug in your grades or the grades you anticipate and see your GPA instantly.

If you give a blessing using your private prayer language, which no one else understands, how can some outsider who has just shown up and has no idea what's going on know when to say, "Amen"? Your blessing might be beautiful, but you have very effectively cut that person out of it. 1Corinthians 14:16-17 (MSG)

Week 2, Day 3

Choosing the Best

Every fall semester I ask my freshmen students to participate in what my campus calls "Get On Board Day." For one day at the beginning of the semester, all the student organizations set up booths on the quadrangle part of our campus and recruit new members. Students can wander through the myriad of tables and learn about all the opportunities for involvement. There are hundreds of organizations to choose from. Political groups, sports enthusiasts, religious organizations and honor societies line up to show off their clubs.

Rachel came by to see me before our class with an armload of flyers and brochures from "Get On Board Day." I think she was a bit overwhelmed, but she seemed to be excited about all the booths she'd visited. "I had no idea there were this many organizations to join. How am I going to have time for all of these?" I couldn't imagine that she would have that much time. Rachel continued, "All of these brochures are from clubs I'd really find interesting, but there are so many!"

I sat down with Rachel and helped her go through the brochures. She had a flyer from a political organization. She had liked the students at the booth, but after more thought, decided that politics wasn't really her strength. Another flyer from an honors society looked promising, and we put that in the stack to keep. Rachel was taking a French class, but the International Students Club required multiple meetings during the month, and Rachel was not sure her aggressive academic schedule would allow her that much free time. Eventually, we narrowed Rachel's choices, and she found the organizations that were best for her and her schedule.

I'm sure you'll find, like Rachel, that there are many good organizations on college campuses. However, not all of those good organizations may be the best for you. Rachel was facing the same dilemma you will face, choosing from among all the good options during your college career. It would be easy if the only choices we needed to make were between bad and good, wouldn't it? But sometimes we have to choose between good and best.

You can't possibly take advantage of all the good options, so make sure you clarify what is important to you. Think about what you value and what goals you have set for yourself this semester in college. Choose organizations that will support those goals and values. If one of your goals is to make all A's this semester, involvement in organizational activities will have to be limited. Choose wisely. Paul taught his believing followers this very concept:

> *Everything is permissible, but not everything is beneficial. Everything is permissible, but not everything is constructive. 1 Cor 10:23 (NIV)*

Rachel found by mid-semester that choosing only two clubs with which to be involved allowed her to keep her grades up and still pursue her interests. I guess I'll be seeing her on the quad next fall recruiting new students!

Use this page to list information about student clubs or

organizations that peak your interest. Use your college's website, visit the Dean of Students Office, or ask other students where a list of student organizations can be found. Find at least three and list some information about them here:

1. Organization Name:

   Requirements to join:

   Purpose of the organization:

   Next meeting time:

2. Organization Name:

   Requirements to join:

   Purpose of the organization:

   Next meeting time:

3. Organization Name:

   Requirements to join:

   Purpose of the organization:

   Next meeting time:

Do any of these organizations fit in with your academic, personal or professional goals? If so, pursue those first.

Rubies:

Believe it or not, a list of organizations on your resume is not very impressive to professional recruiters. What they want to see is that you have taken a leadership role within a club or organization. Being a leader in one or two clubs is better than being a member of ten.

Everything is permissible, but not everything is beneficial. Everything is permissible, but not everything is constructive. 1 Cor 10:23 (NIV)

Week 2, Day 4

Be Encouraged

Maybe you can relate to the story I always tell new freshmen students about my performance on the college entrance exam, ACT. I'm sure you have had to take either the ACT, the SAT or a similar test, and I hope you had a better experience than I did. I made an 18 on the ACT the first and only time I took it. I remember discussing with my mom the option of taking it again, and we both agreed that the likelihood of making a 30 was slim, so I took my 18 and ran. Of course, you can't run very far on an ACT score like that.

I didn't even attempt to apply to a four-year university. Many of my friends were going to the local community college that didn't require an ACT score, so I enrolled in a math course there the summer after my high school graduation. I worked so hard in that class, harder than I've ever worked in any other class. I'd love to tell you that my diligence was inspired by my desire to be highly educated in the ways of algebra and calculus, but my main motivation was fear. I was so scared that my high school habits of meandering lazily through a class would not work in college. I was right, and my hard work paid off. I made an A in that class and proved to myself that I could be successful in college. Many classes followed that first one and I continued to work hard in order to achieve the same success. The work didn't get easier, but I learned how to study smarter in ways that worked for me. For example, I love to read for pleasure, but textbook reading is often a chore. I learned quickly that I needed to read most texts twice in order to retain the information.

I transferred to The University of Alabama after my sophomore year. My ACT score was almost irrelevant because I had a 3.6 grade-point average for my first two years of college. I completed my bachelor's degree with a 3.9 GPA. I found out later that my mom had received a notice from ACT that read something like this: "A student with an ACT score of 18 can expect to be a C student in college." Ha!

If you are starting college with a less than wonderful entrance test score, be encouraged! Your test score does not determine how academically successful you will be in college, because those tests cannot measure your motivation. Your commitment to work hard will determine your success. On the flip side, if you are one of those students with a stellar test score, be careful. I've seen plenty of students with ACT scores of 30+ fail miserably through their first year of college because they didn't take the work seriously.

Commit your works to the Lord
And your plans will be established.
Proverbs 16:3 (NASB)

You can commit even your work in college to the Lord. Pray for perseverance, encouragement, and motivation to work hard in school. Don't be distracted by other students who are not focused on their studies. Trust me; the payoff will come when you are successful on that next test.

- How motivated are you to be successful in college right now? Ask God to help you gain more motivation for your studies:

Commit your works to the Lord
And your plans will be established.
Proverbs 16:3 (NASB)

- What motivates you to study hard? Grades? Rewards?

Rubies:

Remember that tests don't always measure your knowledge on a subject. Don't be defined by your ACT or SAT score. Be motivated to work hard regardless of your entrance exam scores.

Week 2, Day 5

To Minor or Not To Minor

Christina was greatly relieved today when I told her she didn't have to declare a minor to graduate. I think the news made her day. Christina has friends in other colleges who are required to declare minors, but in her college, she doesn't. Sometimes friends can give you well-meaning advice that isn't correct for your particular major or college, so make sure you always check things out with your advisor.

A minor is typically a smaller set of specialized classes in an area other than the one you have chosen as a major. Minors require about 18-22 hours of coursework in the chosen specialty. Ideally, a minor would either support your major program, or it would help you pursue coursework in an area of interest. For example, many of my students who are majoring in marketing will pick up a minor in advertising. The two disciplines work very well together. Other students might choose a minor in art simply because they enjoy drawing or painting.

Christina didn't want to declare a specific minor because she would rather use her elective hours for many different interests. She wants to take courses in a variety of areas, and I think that is a wise decision. Here are some more suggestions about making a minor decision:

- Find out if a minor is required for your degree program. It's important to know early in your academic career, so you can plan accordingly.
- Take the first class required for a minor to see what you think of the subject. You may change your mind after the introductory course.
- If you don't enjoy the coursework, don't choose a minor in that discipline. There is no point in taking classes in a subject you don't enjoy. You will inevitably not use the knowledge professionally.
- Meet with your advisor to discuss the possibilities for a minor. You will also want to discuss the length of the coursework involved and how it will fit into your major program.

Deciding on a minor, or choosing not to declare a minor, is just another opportunity for you to exercise wise decision-making skills. Solomon has so much to say about being wise in Proverbs, including:

Let the wise listen and add to their learning, and let the discerning get guidance. Proverbs 1:5 (NIV)

Getting guidance takes some active participation on your part. Christina did the right thing by making an appointment with her advisor to check on requirements for minors. Don't rely solely on the advice of friends. Ultimately, a minor is not likely to change the direction of your career path, so the decision does not need to weigh heavily on you. But you can certainly find some enjoyment or avoid some hardship by choosing wisely concerning a minor. Take the time to explore all your options.

- Look through your course catalog for possible options for a minor. Investigate disciplines outside of your major. Are there any subjects you find interesting? List a few of them here:

- Would any of these disciplines be a good match for your major? How? Why?

- Choose one or two of these disciplines and look up the requirements for a minor. List those requirements here:

Rubies:

Most minors will require an introduction course to get started. If you are interested in a particular minor, take the first course and see what you think about it. If you decide against the minor, you can always use that first course as an elective.

Let the wise listen and add to their learning, and let the discerning get guidance. Proverbs 1:5 (NIV)

My Notes:

Third Week

Study Skills

Guard well your spare moments. They are like uncut diamonds. Discard them and their value will never be known. Improve them and they will become the brightest gems in a useful life.

- Ralph Waldo Emerson

Week 3, Day 1

Toss It Out

On your way home from class this afternoon, roll down the car window and throw out all your study habits from high school. Don't worry about getting fined for littering, the university cops will totally understand. Wad up those old ideas including cramming right before a test, studying during the lunch period and writing papers the night before the due date. Toss them all out. Everything has changed and your study habits have to change, too.

This week we'll focus on some specific ways that you can improve your study habits and work toward having a successful first semester. And the number one required skill for a successful semester is…

Go to class. Go to every class. Skipping class to go to the pool or hang out with friends is detrimental to your success in any class. Don't depend on friends to get notes or remember details about a lecture. No one else will hear the lecture the same way you will and no one else is concerned about your grades. Every class builds on the one before and it's your responsibility to be there.

Get a B.A.A. Growing up my dad used to tell me and my sister on occasion that we needed a B.A.A. – Barstow Attitude Adjustment. In high school, being the smart kid might not get you admitted to the "in crowd," but in college, academic achievement is cool. Adjust your attitude about studying. Making good grades can open up many doors, and studying subjects you like is actually fun.

Adjust to professor expectations. In high school, students spend a lot of time in class and relatively little time studying outside of class. That time schedule is completely the opposite in college. Professors expect that students will do the vast majority of their work outside of class. Be prepared to spend two hours studying for every one hour you spend in class.

Plan ahead. Successful college students study every day. The all-night cram sessions that seem to be a rite of passage for some students are virtually worthless. Review your notes after class and make corrections while the information is fresh on your mind. Write down upcoming tests and assignments so you can prepare in the days and weeks before the due date. Studying a little along the way is more effective and much less stressful than waiting until the last minute.

Learn more about God. College is much more than textbooks and assignments. It's your life and it's where God wants you right now. If you are studying pre-med, take the time to know more about the Great Physician. Art and sculpture classes on campus can't rival the beauty of creation or the Creator. You might think calculus came from the devil, but in fact all calculations lead back to God. Plan time in your schedule to read your Bible and meditate on God's word.

As you learn more and more how God works,
you will learn how to do your work.
Colossians 1:10 (MSG)

Now there's some advice from Paul that's worth holding on to. Don't toss that one out of the car window!

- Which study habits do you need to "toss out" from high school days?

- Are there any study habits from high school that are worth keeping?

As you learn more and more how God works, you will learn how to do your work. Colossians 1:10 (MSG)

- What can you do to learn more about God this semester

Rubies:

Make sure to get enough sleep along with improving your study skills. Students need about seven hours of sleep to be effective participants in and out of the classroom. Save the late nights for celebrating after the work is done.

Week 3, Day 2

Write It Down

I always tried to beat my sister, Leslie, to the mailbox when we were growing up. Exciting things came in the mailbox – letters, cards, or even a package. I kept quite a few pen pals through the years until I went to college, and the anticipation of another letter with my name on it kept me looking out for the mailman every afternoon. I still have boxes of letters from my friends in junior high and high school. Guess what we all have now? An inbox full of emails and a mailbox full of junk!

The discipline of writing seems to be a thing of the past. We all bang away on the keyboard or laptop now instead of using stationary. Email and text are great for sending quick notes, but our hands get tired after writing a few sentences in a notebook. Students struggle in the classroom to take effective notes during lectures because they're out of practice. Lecture notes can be your lifeline for any class. Everyone can improve their note-taking skills by following some simple guidelines.

Keep it neat. Notes from a class that you can't read the next day are useless. Don't worry about using too much paper. Space out your writing so you can make corrections later. Use only one side of the paper to keep your notes neat and to have space for including extra notes if needed.

Use abbreviations. You'll have to shorten words and use symbols in most classes. Lectures go quickly, so learn to improvise. Script is much faster than print. Make yourself a key in the margins so you can remember what your abbreviations mean! Experienced students know you can't possibly write every word the professor says, so make your own shortcuts in order to get the most from the lecture.

Think like the professor. Professors give verbal hints about what is most important. If the professor is interested in a particular topic, you can bet it will be on a test. She may also emphasize points by repeating them, speaking louder or more slowly, or by even saying, "This is important."

Don't rely on others. Many colleges make lecture notes available for purchase. I would advise you to use these only as an *addition* to your own notes. You are the one in the classroom and you can hear what the professor emphasized in the lecture. What if the person selling notes is in another section with a different professor? Take and study your own notes.

Review ASAP. Read through your notes after class as soon as possible. You'll want to fill in gaps and make corrections while the information is still fresh on your mind.

None of us gets too many hand-written letters in the mailbox these days, but God has written many letters just for you. Putting words on paper is still the most effective form of communication. When Solomon had something important to say, he thought the best idea was to write it down.

Write this at the top of your list: Get Understanding! Throw your arms around her—believe me, you won't regret it.
Proverbs 4:7 (MSG)

- What types of note-taking skills did you utilize in high school?

- What changes need to be made now that you are in college-level courses?

- Brainstorm some ideas for using abbreviations. Think about your current courses. What shortcuts can you use to be most efficient when taking notes?

As you learn more and more how God works, you will learn how to do your work. Colossians 1:10 (MSG)

Rubies:

I think 3-ring binders are great for classes that require many pages of notes. You can take the pages out and rearrange at will. Binders also allow for adding handouts that go with a particular set of notes. Spiral notebooks don't allow for as much flexibility.

Week 3, Day 3

Stay on Course

The greatest study advice ever given boils down to this: follow the directions. For some professors, it doesn't matter at all how much you know about the subject if you did the assignment in the wrong font, turned it in at the wrong time, or didn't complete the required number of pages. You might know every detail about the subject and still receive a below-average grade.

One semester I had a professor who was meticulous about grading assignments. He clearly listed on the syllabus that all typed assignments were to be turned in with one-inch margins, a maximum font of 12, and each had specific length requirements. If any hand-written assignments were required, only blue ink would be acceptable. How serious could he be? I looked over the directions, but didn't really think anyone would be so picky about grading. Surely if I got all the answers right it wouldn't matter if my margins were a little wider, right? Wrong! The first assignment I received back from this professor was covered in red marks, and I got a C- as a grade. My content was right, but I didn't follow the directions given for the assignment.

As a teacher, I understand the reason for directions a little better than I did as a student. I teach almost 200 students each fall semester. If I didn't have specific guidelines for assignments, I would get all kinds of crazy submissions. Reading a paper written in neon green ink gives you a headache, and don't I know it. Each professor has a reason for the guidelines required for assignments, so remember that part of your grade will depend on following those directions.

As a Christian, you've been given a specific set of directions for developing your spiritual walk. In His Word, God has provided a road map for your life. Of course, you have to read the directions to know how to complete the assignment. More wisdom from the book of Psalms:

You're blessed when you stay on course,
walking steadily on the road revealed by
GOD. You're blessed when you follow his
directions, doing your best to find him.
Psalm 119:1-2 (MSG)

How can a young person live a clean life?
By carefully reading the map of your
Word. I'm single-minded in pursuit of you;
don't let me miss the road signs you've
posted. Psalm 119:9-10 (MSG)

Following directions in your coursework is important, but following God's directions for your life is imperative. The only way to know God's direction for your life is to read His manual. Through daily Bible reading and prayer, you can discern direction for school, your personal life, family issues and anything else that comes up along the way. God's directions are always true, righteous and holy. They won't lead you down the wrong path. Be blessed by staying on course and following His guide.

The best part is that God doesn't mind a little neon green ink on his assignment. Be colorful and don't worry about the margins!

- Have you ever lost points on an assignment because you didn't follow the directions? What happened?

- What can you do today to make sure that you're following God's directions for your life? Read the Bible? Pray? Make a commitment here to follow God's directions in these and other ways.

You're blessed when you stay on course, walking steadily on the road revealed by God. You're blessed when you follow his directions, do ing your best to find him. Psalm 119:1-2 (MSG)

Rubies:

It's very easy to lose points on essay questions if you don't follow the directions. A teacher may ask you to explain, discuss, compare, list or analyze. Each of these directions is very different. Pay attention to what the teacher is asking for in an essay question. Don't explain when you've been directed to compare.

Week 3, Day 4

Mathematical Survival 101

What a blessing to have one friend who is a bona fide math genius. Pam and I live in adjoining neighborhoods and walk most nights for exercise. As we circle the block, she calculates our mileage, figures my taxes and helps me keep up with my budget. I can barely total those figures with my calculator.

Pam is a high school math teacher and knows that math is a tough subject for many college students. The only secret to being successful in math, or any other class, is to be diligent in your studies.

Remember: the duller the ax, the harder
the work; Use your head: The more
brains, the less muscle.
Ecclesiastes 10:10 (MSG)

Professor Pam has years of experience tutoring college students in math and related subjects. Here are some of her suggestions for surviving your math class:

- Attend class every day. Don't try to play catch-up. Math topics build on each other. If you miss one topic, you will probably miss the next one.
- Do ALL homework problems assigned. Homework provides an opportunity for you to practice and apply the ideas from class. If you

don't use it, you lose it. Practice will help refine your understanding of the concepts and keep you from losing "careless" points.

- Ask questions. If you don't ask, you can't get the answer.
- Talk to your professor. Show the professor that you are serious about your studies by talking with him/her outside of class or when you are having trouble.
- Study, Study, Study. Don't buy into the idea that you can't study for a math test. You study by reworking homework problems and checking your answers against the answers in the back of the book.
- Don't cram. Math concepts take time to develop. You cannot learn five or six sections of material in one day or even one week. Study a little each night.
- Don't try to take a math test when you're tired. Don't spend the nights before the tests out partying with friends or stay up all night studying. Spend the night before the test reviewing the areas that have previously been difficult for you. Then, get some rest.
- Ask for help. Use any study sessions provided by the department or the teacher. Hire a tutor or see if your college provides tutors free of charge. If you need help, find it!

Implementing Pam's suggestions will give you a better chance for success, but ultimately the amount of work you put in will determine the results. Sharpen the ax so you won't have to use all your muscle. You'll need some of that muscle for science and history!

- Have you struggled with math in the past? Which classes or parts of mathematics have been the toughest for you?

- What services are available at your college for students struggling in math?

- Which of Pam's suggestions can you implement immediately to ensure success on your next math assignment? Write a commitment below to implement one or all of Pam's suggestions.

Remember: the duller the ax, the harder the work; Use your head: The more brains, the less muscle. Ecclesiastes 10:10 (MSG)

Rubies:

Most university math departments have a math lab where students can study and get help with difficult problems. Find out if your university has a math lab and use it!

Week 3, Day 5

A Time for Everything

The wise Old Testament teacher, King Solomon, wrote extensively in Ecclesiastes about how God has made a time for everything under the sun. Read Ecclesiastes 3:1-8. There is a time for birth and death, war and peace, even love and hate. God has already determined a time for all the events in your life, including your time in college.

Time, and how you use it, will be one of your greatest assets or one of your biggest challenges in college. Students are notorious for wasting time, and even more notorious for regretting it. Time management skills are essential to making other study skills, such as note taking and textbook reading, most effective. Here are some suggestions for getting the most out of your time.

Take notes on yourself. Write down for one week how you spend your time. Include sleeping, watching TV, hanging out with friends, class and study time. Analyze how many hours you are spending in leisure time as compared to work or study time. Remember, each class requires approximately two hours of study time.

Combine activities. Find ways to do two things at once. Pay bills while watching TV, straighten up your room while talking on the phone or catch up with friends by spending lunch time together. Take advantage of the opportunity to get more done in less time.

Maximize time between classes. It's easy to waste an hour between classes. You might not be able to get off campus for your weekly grocery shopping, but you can do small errands. This is also a great opportunity to look over notes from class, catch up on an assignment or update your calendar. Getting a few things done between classes will free you up for fun later.

Say "No." You can't be the president of every club and you can't go to every party. It's just not possible. Pick out the activities that are most important to you and say "Yes" to those. Spending time on too many activities will drain the energy you need for the commitments that are most important.

Practice your ABC's. The ABC method of prioritizing responsibilities has been used by college students for years. Make a list of your activities for the day then divide them based on priority. A's are the most important and must be completed by the end of the day. B's are important, but might be able to wait until later in the week. C priorities are the least pressing and only need to be completed within the month. Start with your A priorities and work your way down. This method should give you some perspective on which obligations warrant the most attention.

Enjoy your work. Have fun even while you are prioritizing all your commitments. Cut out the ones that are unnecessary and are a drain on your schedule. Solomon continues with his wisdom in Ecclesiastes 3:13 (NIV):

That everyone may eat and drink, and find
satisfaction in all his toil—
this is the gift of God.

Try to estimate how much time you spend doing each of these activities in a typical week:

Time in class:	______ hrs.
Studying:	______ hrs.
Working, part-time job:	______ hrs.
Going to and from class:	______ hrs.
Extracurricular activities (clubs, Bible study, etc.)	______ hrs.
Exercising:	______ hrs.
Sleeping:	______hrs.
Preparing and eating meals:	______ hrs.
Running errands:	______ hrs.
Hanging out with friends:	______ hrs.
Grooming, "getting ready to go":	______ hrs.
Time on-line:	______ hrs.
Total:	______ hrs.

Are you using more than the 168 hours in a week?

Rubies:

Most people have a part of the day during which they are at their best. Mine is definitely not early morning, although I still have to go to work at 8:00 A.M.! If you are more alert at certain times during the day, schedule your toughest classes at that time if you can. Give yourself every advantage to be successful.

There is a time for everything, and a season for every activity under heaven. Ecclesiastes 3:1 (NIV)

My Notes:

Fourth Week

All Hard Work Brings a Profit

When we long for life without difficulties, remind us that oaks grow strong in contrary winds and diamonds are made under pressure.

- Peter Marshall

Week 4, Day 1

Idle Hands

Our world is full of interesting dichotomies, isn't it? Sometimes the craziest things go together and work out well. Like people, for instance. I think it's so funny to see a big burly guy in black leather get off his Harley and take the hand of a sweet-looking girl in a pink sundress. They don't look like they go together, but opposites must attract. Maybe the most unlikely candidate for the student government association is the one who wins by a landslide, or the shiest girl you know is the one everybody else wants to ask to the party. Things like that happen all the time. God has a great sense of humor.

Bethany, one of my students from a class I taught a few semesters back, came in today to go over her schedule and plan for registration. As we looked over her grades, it was obvious that in some semesters her grades were much better than in others. I said, "Was there something happening in these semesters when your grades were not so great? Were you having any problems at that time?" Bethany's eyes got really big, like she'd just realized something important, and she said, "Believe it or not, my best grades happened during the semesters when I was working part time and I was so busy!" I had heard this scenario many times, but it had evidently just occurred to her. She continued, "Can you believe that when I had the most going on outside of class I made my best grades?" Well, yes I can.

I know it doesn't seem to fit – like black leather and pink sundresses – but some of the most successful students in college are also some of the busiest. People get more done when they have a lot to do and that goes for college students, too. Don't get me wrong – I'm not advocating that you overload your schedule. There is certainly a point at which you'll have too much on your plate. But one of the best homespun remedies for a lagging GPA is putting a limit on idle time. A little idle time inevitably turns into a lot of idle time. There are several warnings in the Bible about idleness including,

If a man is lazy, the rafters sag; if his hands are idle, the house leaks. Ecclesiastes 10:18 (NIV)

We hear that some among you are idle. They are not busy; they are busybodies. 2 Thessalonians 3:11(NIV)

A student with too much idle time is usually a student who is not keeping up with his coursework – the house is leaking. Some great ideas for filling idle time include getting a part-time job, joining a club, volunteering in the community, getting involved in a church or campus Bible study or serving as an officer of a student organization. It will take a little experimenting to discover how much extra-curricular involvement is too much. Don't overload. Dichotomies work well in life all the time. A part-time job or a little more activity could actually give your school work a boost.

- What are some clubs or organizations you could get involved with in your college?

- Think about your activities over the past week. When did you have the most open time?

If a man is lazy, the rafters sag; if his hands are idle, the house leaks. Ecclesiastes 10:18 (NIV)

- What kind of jobs do your friends have? Can they help you get a part time job?

Rubies:

Find the Student Employment Office on your campus and see what jobs are listed. If you don't find anything right away, check back in a week for any new postings.

Week 4, Day 2

A Path of Briers or a Smooth Road

My students are losing their minds! Or maybe I'm the one whose mind is missing. The semester is over around here, and grades are posted. Guess what that means? The students who goofed off all semester are lined up outside my door, tissues in hand or angry parents in tow, begging to find out how they can repair the damage. Oh my, how distressed they are! Some are despondent, some are hysterical, and some are going to spend the next semester at home with their parents.

One of my favorite students had a really rough semester. She e-mailed me repeatedly yesterday with one anxiety-ridden message after another. When she called this morning, I relayed the message that concern of this magnitude about her coursework during the semester would have resulted in all A's. She readily agreed, and hopefully has learned a lesson.

There are a few things you need to know before you think that a bad semester can be easily recovered:

- Your grades are permanent. In most cases, the grades you make are the grades you have to live with – no way out.
- A low grade point average can be difficult to pull up if you have acquired a significant number of earned hours.
- Grades taken at an institution other than your home college really do transfer, so don't blow off summer classes or classes you take at the local community college.

I'm glad to report that most of my students are celebrating the results of a semester of hard work. They are making summer plans and enjoying a hard-earned rest instead of being stressed out about their recent grade report. The road ahead is smooth. Proverbs confirms the reward of diligence:

The path of lazy people is overgrown with briers; the diligent walk down a smooth road. Proverbs 15:19 (MSG)

I chose this verse specifically because of the word "lazy." The vast majority of my students who struggle with grades do so because they don't work hard, not because they are unable to do the work. You wouldn't be in college right now if you couldn't handle the academic rigor. College is hard, but it's not too hard.

Regret is tough. My students who are reaping the results of a semester spent in fun and games would say it was definitely not worth it. Their paths are overgrown with briers.

I hope you are reading this before you've had a chance to experience this kind of regret over a semester. If so, be mature enough to learn from someone else's mistakes and make the necessary corrections in your current semester before it's too late. Set yourself up to enjoy a smooth road at the end of this semester. Oops, gotta go –someone else with a handful of tissues is standing at my door…

- Are you working hard this semester? Take an inventory of your semester to this point and write down any thoughts about your performance:

- What changes do you need to make, if any?

- At the end of this semester, will your path be covered in briers or will your road be smooth?

The path of lazy people is overgrown with briers; the diligent walk down a smooth road. Proverbs 15:19 (MSG)

Rubies:

Guard against the influence of friends who lure you away from your work. Make a conscious effort to become friends with fellow students who share your desire for academic success. Encourage each other to stay on track.

Week 4, Day 3

There's No Time to Lose

Can you guess one of the top barriers to student success? I was going to tell you all about it here, but I really just don't feel like making the effort right now. There are so many fun things I could be doing, and I think I'll just put off telling you about it until later when I have more time. Sound familiar? Procrastination is a huge barrier to student success and a hard habit to break.

Students have more unstructured time in college than they've ever had before. Notice I didn't say "free time." You're spending fewer hours in class than you did in high school, but you have much more responsibility and much more homework. The expectation level for your performance is higher now, and it's extremely easy to get behind.

Here's what usually happens: you roll out of bed for your 10:00 class without enough time to eat breakfast. So by the time morning classes end at noon, you're starving. A friend suggests grabbing lunch at the student union and that sounds like a good idea. While you're there, you see no fewer than 20 of your closest friends, and, after catching up on all the latest gossip, you have to run to your two o'clock class. Classes are finally over by five o'clock, and then it's time to eat again. After dinner in the cafeteria, someone suggests a movie. Of course, that sounds like lots more fun than homework, so you agree. And it goes on and on until you finally crash at midnight and start the whole thing over again the next day.

See how easy it is to get behind in just a few days with an undisciplined approach to your schedule? Don't be moved along through your day by suggestions of others for good times and fun. There will always – always! – be something more fun to do than homework and projects. You can't put off school work every time something fun comes along and be successful in college.

Solomon is considered to be the wisest man who ever lived. Read what he wrote in Proverbs:

Don't procrastinate – there's no time to lose... So how long are you going to laze around doing nothing? How long before you get out of bed? A nap here, a nap there, a day off here, a day off there, sit back, take it easy – do you know what comes next? Just this: You can look forward to a dirt-poor life, poverty your permanent houseguest!
Proverbs 6:4, 9-11(MSG)

These verses might sound a little extreme in relation to putting off some homework, but Solomon knew how quickly a little procrastination can turn into poverty. Avoid this pitfall by making a plan for each day. Make a list of all the homework you need to complete, errands you need to finish and projects you need to start. Don't let others influence your time and distract you from completing your goals for the day. You'll be surprised by how good it feels to reach all those goals, even if you still have to crash at midnight.

- Take a look at your class syllabi and make a plan for the week. List at least one major goal for each day that will help you accomplish the ultimate goal of success!

Monday:

Tuesday:

Wednesday:

Thursday:

Friday:

Don't procrastinate – there's no time to lose... Proverbs 6:4

Rubies:

Get a calendar and plot out assignments for the semester. Check it daily to make sure you're on track. Use only one calendar for personal and school entries – multiple calendars are confusing and time consuming.

Week 4, Day 4

No Excuses!

The very best advertising campaigns in the world are displayed on the inside of New York City subway trains. I travel with students every year to The Big Apple, and I am always amazed at the creative slogans on the trains – most of which are really funny. There isn't much conversation on the subway, so most patrons have little to do other than read the signs posted overhead. On a recent subway trip, I saw what will probably be my all-time favorite subway advertisement.

The poster advertised an art institute, but its intent wasn't apparent right away. Across the top of the poster the words stood out in bold: Stop – Stop – Stop – Start! Under each "Stop" there was an excuse in quotations for why a person couldn't pursue art school: "Anyone can throw paint on a canvas and call it art," or "Painting is my hobby but you can't make money chasing after your hobbies." Under the "Start" was the logo for the art institute. I thought it was a great ad!

Imagine what your college version of this poster would look like. Stop – "I don't have enough time to complete all these assignments." Stop – "I'm not as smart as other people in my class, so I can't possibly get a good grade." Stop – "These classes are too hard!" Stop – "I made a bad grade on the first test, so I might as well stop trying in this class." There may be many other excuses we could add to this list, but these are some of the ones I hear often.

Now imagine what God would say under "Start!"

The lazy person is full of excuses...
Proverbs 26:13 (NLT)

We command them to get to work immediately – no excuses, no arguments – and earn their own keep. 2 Thessalonians 3:12 (MSG)

God's message to you for this semester of college is, "Get to work and make no excuses!" Negative self-talk can do real damage to your success in school. Working overtime to come up with excuses about why you can't be successful is a waste of time and will eventually lead you to believe those excuses. I am often convinced that students work harder at getting out of tasks than they would if they just buckled down and completed the assignment. Don't you remember doing this as a child? Finding excuses to get out of cleaning your room took up more time than the actual cleaning. It's time to leave childish things in the past.

The truth is there are very few college students who are not capable of being successful academically. The reason you were accepted to the university you're attending is because the educators there knew you could do the work. Universities don't admit students who don't have the potential to be successful. However, the administrators at your university can't judge from your application alone how you will use your potential. So get to it and show everyone, yourself included, that you are a success. No excuses!

- What kind of excuses are you using for procrastinating or for poor performance? Be honest!!

- Now turn those excuses into positives. Rewrite a few of them here to reflect how you can change something negative into something positive:

The lazy person is full of excuses… Proverbs 26:13 (NLT)

Rubies:

Find an accountability partner who can help call your attention to any excuses you might be using for poor habits or performance. Don't get irritated with a good friend who helps you out in this department. Take the constructive criticism and use it to become more successful.

Week 4, Day 5

Great Gifts

I want to encourage you during this first semester to cultivate an attitude of viewing your college education as a gift. For the past twelve years, whether you attended a public or private school, your education has been a right, guaranteed by the laws that govern our country. Our government has declared that all citizens will have the opportunity for primary and secondary education. The opportunity to pursue an education at the college level is not included in that mandate. A college education is a gift.

The ability to see your college experience as a gift will impact how gratefully you embrace it, how well you endure it and how responsible you become for your own success. Students who think of their college education as a "right" wait on others for instruction, assuming if there is something they need to know, the information will be provided. Trust me, no one with a crystal ball will knock on your residence hall door. Students who think of their college education as a gift become proactive and go after the information they need. These students are also involved in giving back to their university through service or volunteerism.

Being responsible for this gift requires some effort on your part. Every college or university has a published list of student responsibilities, and you should become familiar with those expectations. Some of the most general responsibilities include the following:

- Understand university/college policies, procedures and curricula. Obtain, review and keep a copy of your college catalog and student handbook.
- Be an honest and ethical member of your academic community. Don't cheat, plagiarize or put other students at risk.
- Act in a timely manner. Be on time, honor deadlines, don't procrastinate.
- Stay abreast of your academic progress. Your schedule is just that – YOUR schedule. Don't rely on your advisor to choose all your classes. Participate in the process of your own education.
- Ask questions and seek help when necessary. No one will know you need help unless you are bold enough to ask. Be assertive!
- Keep an open mind. There are so many new experiences waiting for you – don't miss any of them.
- Make a connection with at least one faculty or staff member. These people can help you become a better learner and will be your best cheerleader.

Whew! You've got a lot to do, right? Don't let this slide. Make an appointment with your advisor if you don't know where to start. Of course, the best place to start is with your own attitude about your education. Great gifts and great responsibility go hand in hand. That's how you know it's worth the work.

Great gifts mean great responsibilities;
greater gifts, greater responsibilities!
Luke 12:48b (MSG)

- Look up your college's Student Rights and Responsibilities page in your catalog or handbook. List any items below that are not included in my list.

Great gifts mean great responsibilities; greater gifts, greater responsibilities! Luke 12:48b (MSG)

- What do you need to do this semester to act in a timely manner? Do you need to make an appointment with your advisor? If so, list here who you need to contact and the date of your meeting.

Rubies:

Most colleges have a "Student Responsibilities" component for financial aid and for student organizations. If you are involved in either, it would be a good idea to check out those lists as well.

My Notes:

Fifth Week

All Different Kinds of People

The most precious jewels are not made of
stone, but of flesh…
- Robert Ludlum

Week 5, Day 1

All Different Kinds of People

Dianne thought she had seen it all. A few weeks into the semester, she stopped me after class and said, "I can't believe how many different kinds of people there are here. And I'm from the city!" Dianne grew up and went to high school in a big city with plenty of cultural diversity. Her neighborhood was home to people from many different races and ethnicities. Still, she was amazed at the varied backgrounds of her fellow classmates.

Whether you're from the big city or a country community, you're going to meet people from races, creeds and cultures you have never heard of. It's a great opportunity to learn about the rest of the world, but it can be a little intimidating, too. I think some students avoid making friends from different backgrounds because they don't even know how to get started. Here are some tips:

Avoid assumptions. There is as much diversity within race and ethnic groups as there is between them. When talking or socializing with someone different from you, try to be cognizant of any stereotypes you might hold. Just approach them as a fellow human being and classmate.

Listen and learn. I bet you don't agree with your closest friends all the time, so you can't expect to always agree with people of other religions or cultures. That's perfectly okay. Include tolerance and a willingness to listen in any discussion. You'll get to know what makes people tick and they will get to know the same about you. Don't force your views or opinions on people who have grown up differently than you. Through polite conversation, you'll be heard.

Be sensitive. Use the appropriate term when referring to groups of people and be specific when possible. For example, Asian people are not "Oriental." Oriental is a term for rugs or vases, not for people. When appropriate, use terms like Japanese American or Native American. When in doubt, just ask someone for the appropriate term. In most cases, your willingness to get it right will be appreciated.

You'll hear a lot about diversity and tolerance in college. You might think that it's really no big deal. However, learning to be tolerant of others while in college will serve you well for the rest of your life. The workplace is becoming more and more diverse, and your professional success after school could be influenced by your ability to work well with people from a variety of backgrounds.

Being tolerant of others doesn't mean you have to compromise your own beliefs. You'll actually have more opportunities to share your faith and make a greater impact doing so if you are open to learning about others. Paul has some great advice for city dwellers and small town folks alike:

Therefore... walk in a manner worthy of the calling with which you have been called, with all humility and gentleness, with patience, showing tolerance for one another in love. Ephesians 4: 1-2 (NASB)

- How would you define the term "diversity"?

- Have you witnessed incidents of intolerance on the part of your classmates toward people from other cultures or religions?

- How would you feel if you were a minority at your college or university?

Therefore... walk in a manner worthy of the calling with which you have been called, with all humility and gentleness, with patience, showing tolerance for one another in love. Ephesians 4: 1-2 (NASB)

Rubies:

There's no better diversity training than studying abroad. Seek out opportunities on your campus to spend a semester in another country. If this is not an option for you, seek out international students on your campus and coach them in English or study skills.

Week 5, Day 2

Treat Everyone with Dignity

The poor guy who just left my office learned a hard lesson today. I want to share it with you because it's a good one. My office is located right behind the reception desk in our main student services office. Usually, that's not a good thing, because I hear everything that's going on out there – phones ringing, people chatting and the fax machine beeping. I also overhear most of the conversations that take place between the students and my co-workers.

A student came to the front desk and demanded to see an advisor. He was obviously upset. I was finishing up with another student in my office, but I overheard the exchange at the front desk. Our receptionist informed the angry student that all the advisors were presently with other students and asked him to wait for a few minutes until someone became available. The student was belligerent and nasty to our receptionist, using language unfit for professional places.

In order to stop the mayhem, I leaned over my desk, caught his eye and gestured for him to come into my office. He sneered at our receptionist and said, "Lori will see me," as if he'd won the fight of the century with the ultimate enemy. He was all smiles and sweetness when he got to my door. How do you think I responded? I can assure you he will not forget. We eventually solved his academic problem, but only after we had a generous heart-to-heart discussion about how he treated the people who are working for him in my office.

Why am I telling you about this incident? Everyone who works at your college deserves to be treated with dignity and respect regardless of their station or position of influence. This student temporarily forgot (giving him the benefit of the doubt) that he can catch more flies with honey.

Out of respect for Christ, be courteously
reverent to one another.
Ephesians 5:21 (MSG)

Secretaries, for example, are some of the most influential people in an office. My boss listens carefully to what his secretary has to say and takes her opinion under advisement regularly. If you want to get in to see my boss, you have to go through his secretary. She can make it more or less difficult for any of our students to get what they need. In many cases, the secretary of a department has better information than the professors.

In addition, my co-workers and I have a great appreciation for our custodians. They have the keys to locked doors, jumper cables and storage boxes; and they give great directions because they know every nook of this building. Don't overlook these people. As a Christian college student, set an example in how you relate to those who are often overlooked around your campus, showing dignity and respect to everyone.

- Pay attention today to people who might go unnoticed in your college buildings. Did you cross paths with a custodian or a receptionist? Where?

- What could you say to one of these valuable workers that would brighten their day?

Out of respect for Christ, be courteously reverent to one another.
Ephesians 5:21 (MSG)

Rubies:

Meet the secretary in your department. If you need forms signed by a faculty member who seems scarce, the secretary can usually get the job done.

Week 5, Day 3

Roommates

I've seen plenty of commercials that featured college students, but one has always been my favorite. Two girls are going to college for the first time. One girl arrives in her residence hall room first. She's dressed completely in black – black fingernails, black hair, black lipstick. She looks up to find her new roommate standing at the door wearing a pink plaid skirt, bow in her hair, carrying a backpack with flowers all over it. One would think these girls have nothing in common, but they brought the same laptop to school so they find some common ground.

Are you nervous about your new roommate? Even if you are living with a good friend, you may have some concerns about getting along while sharing a kitchen and a bathroom. As a matter of fact, most people would say it's harder to room with good friends than with strangers. Friends tend to take advantage of one another assuming that their friendship will survive a lack of consideration. I had a roommate once who cleaned up pots and pans in the kitchen before she ate the meal she prepared. The food was on the table and she was scrubbing a pot. I never could get used to that. And I'm sure there were things I did that drove her crazy, too. You're comfortable sharing your space with family, but roommates are a new experience.

Jesus told his followers to, "Love your neighbor as yourself" in Luke 10:27b (NIV). This goes for roommates, too! Here are a few suggestions on dealing with new roommates:

- Try to resist your first impression, especially if it's negative. Give the relationship a chance to develop.
- Remember, college roommates do not have to be best friends. However, they do need to be considerate and polite. Make the effort, even if your roommate has forgotten her manners.
- Don't worry if you don't click right away. Sometimes it takes time to get to know someone. You might find common interests later.
- Sit down with your new roommate and discuss the big issues before they become conflicts: paying bills, cleaning chores, quiet hours, visitors (especially boyfriends) and grocery shopping.
- Communicate with your roommate. Don't keep concerns bottled up until you explode in anger or frustration. Express your frustrations in a civil, polite manner. And take it well when your roommate does the same.

A roommate can be a big asset during the first year of college. She can be a sounding board for your opinions and ideas, an encouragement during test time and maybe even a good friend. It's great to have someone close by when you want to hang out, stress out or go out. Keep in mind that having a good roommate is only half the equation. Being a good roommate is your responsibility. If you are into punk music, but your roommate is into country, give the relationship a chance. After all, college is all about new experiences.

- Make a list of some things you need to discuss with your new roommate. Include chores related to keeping up your apartment or room, rules related to visitors and quiet hours.

- How can you pray for your roommate every day?

Love the Lord your God with all your heart and with all your soul and with all your strength and with all your mind; and Love your neighbor as yourself.
Luke 10:27 (NIV)

Rubies:

Being a good roommate means paying attention to the things your roommate values. If she needs quiet to be able to study, honor that and keep your noise to a minimum. Looking out for her will make her want to be considerate to you.

Week 5, Day 4

It's All About Respect

Professors. Even now I can remember the ones I absolutely loved and the ones who struck fear in my heart each time I entered their classroom. I've had great professors, and I've had professors who were sorely in need of a retirement plan, and you will, too. Most students have at least one professor who is completely intimidating. Many times these professors are perceived as gruff or arrogant, which makes the very idea of approaching them scary. Students are hesitant to approach even those professors who are well liked, because they seem busy or just too intelligent to relate on a student's level.

Every student must quickly learn to communicate effectively with professors, and it all comes down to respect. The professor is in a position of authority over a student regardless of whether or not you agree on personal or political issues, whether or not you like the structure of the class and whether or not you think the professor is a nice person. None of that stuff matters when it comes to learning to communicate. Here are some pointers for starting a conversation with a professor:

- Begin by introducing yourself and offering a handshake.
- Tell the professor where you are from and inquire about his/her hometown. People like to talk about home.
- Ask if you can drop by during posted office hours if you have a question or concern about the class.

This should get things off to a nice start with your professors. Believe it or not, most professors want you to be successful and are available to help you when you need it. At the same time, professors are very busy with work outside of the classroom. Here are some classic "don'ts" when talking with a professor:

- Never start a conversation with "Are you busy?" They are.
- Never drop by the office and say, "I've come by here seven times in the past week, and you're never here!" It sounds accusatory.
- Never misspell a professor's name or use Mr./Ms. instead of Dr.
- Never address a professor by their first name unless they offer – and maybe even wait until they offer twice.

Professors can be wonderful resources both in and out of the classroom during your academic career. You'll eventually need a reference from a professor, and now is the time to start cultivating a few of those relationships. Not all professors are intimidating, so approach at least one this semester and try to find some common ground.

Most importantly, be respectful regardless of how the professor responds to you. There is never a reason to be discourteous toward a professor. Peter said it best when he wrote, "Show proper respect to everyone" in 1 Peter 2:17 (NIV). Great advice! I feel certain Peter would have included intimidating college professors in his definition of "everyone."

- Is there a particular professor this semester you find intimidating? Use the space below to write out some examples of conversation starters you could use to introduce yourself:

Show proper respect to everyone.
1 Peter 2:17 (NIV)

Rubies:

Ask your professors about their hobbies or interests. You could discover common interests and find that you have much to talk about.

Week 5, Day 5

Don't Give Up Meeting Together

I hope by now you have found a church home and college group in your new town (or have joined the college group in your home church). There are plenty of opportunities on campus for students to join a weekly Bible study or group with which they can socialize. Perhaps you have attended church services with friends or have already met other Christians who are active in a local church. For many students, that's just not the case, and they have to find a new church home on their own.

I didn't leave my hometown to go to college, but I essentially left my home church. I made a huge mistake, and I want to encourage you not to do the same. I showed up to the college department Bible study meetings occasionally, but never made a connection there. Do you know why? All those hypocrites! It just makes me groan in embarrassment to think back on it. I got terribly sidetracked by the other people in my college group. It seemed to me that some of the most involved members of the class were the same ones out partying all weekend and drinking. I'd hear rumors about what they were doing on Friday night and then see them looking all prim and proper on Sunday morning. I let the actions of others dictate my own church attendance – or used them as an excuse to stay away. Paul admonishes in Hebrews 10:25 (NIV):

Let us not give up meeting together, as some are in the habit of doing, but let us encourage one another – and all the more as you see the Day approaching.

There are two specific directions in this verse. The first is obvious – don't quit going to church. People who get on your nerves or who are acting out rebellion in their personal lives are not excuses for staying away from a congregation of believers. It's imperative for your own spiritual health to be around other Christians and to seek out sound biblical teaching. I should have been focusing on Jesus and our relationship instead of what everyone else in my class was doing. I certainly didn't have a clean slate myself.

It might be easy to generalize that the only person I hurt by staying away from church was me, but the second part of this verse says otherwise. We are to "encourage one another" in our faith. Not only did I give up the encouragement I could have received from others at church, I gave up on my responsibility to encourage others.

You can make a difference to someone in any congregation, large or small. Find a church home and be faithful in your attendance and involvement. Most college students struggle with living out their spiritual beliefs in everyday life. When you see that happening with a fellow church member, build them up and help them stay on track. You'll need the same encouragement eventually, and when the time comes your church family will be the first to back you up

- Are you using any excuses to avoid meeting together with other Christians? Get honest about it here and then pray for God to change your attitude:

- Do some research and find out about Christian organizations on campus. Make a list here of the groups and when they meet.

Let us not give up meeting together, as some are in the habit of doing, but let us encourage one another – and all the more as you see the Day approaching. Hebrews 10:25 (NIV)

Rubies:

Ask a friend to go to a church service or a college group with you for the first time. It's much more comfortable to know that someone is there with you instead of going alone. Then you can encourage each other to make church attendance a priority!

My Notes:

Sixth Week

Relationships

Give crowns and pounds and guineas
But not your heart away;
Give pearls away and rubies,
But keep your fancy free.
- A.E. Housman

Week 6, Day 1

Waiting and Dating

Natasha reveals the state of her dating life on her T-shirts. On Monday she'll wear something bright and sunny with the word "Princess" or "Super Star" on the front. By Thursday she'll show up to work in our office wearing all black with "Boys Lie!" printed in large script across her shirt. Relationships. They are tough at any age but especially during college.

Are you expecting to find your one true love in college? If you're like most freshman women, you probably started checking out the guys from your first moments on campus. You look around and think, *That one's too short* or *I don't like his haircut* and start the weed-out process before you've even been introduced. I'm sure some women think college is where they are supposed to find a husband. The truth is that relatively few women graduate from college with an engagement ring and a booked chapel.

The expectation of finding true and perfect love in college can lead to feelings of disappointment if you don't find Mr. Right within the first few weeks on campus. Or those expectations can lead to jumping into an unhealthy relationship too quickly. The notion that any boyfriend is better than no boyfriend seems to be a rampant concept among college women.

I remember a close friend in college who decided that it was obviously God's will for her to be single because she had not found a significant relationship by the time she was 21 years old. It seems silly now –

especially in light of the fact that she's not only married, but has 4 children! At the time, my friend was convinced of her life-long sentence to singleness, so she let out a dramatic sigh and assumed the position of a martyr.

Be careful not to let your disappointment over college relationships develop into bitterness. The martyr complex is definitely not the way to attract supportive friends, much less suitors! Instead, focus your attention on developing your relationship with God. Find your comfort and encouragement in the most significant relationship you will ever have in your life.

May your unfailing love be my comfort,
according to your promise to your servant.
Psalm 119:76 (NIV)

I know it's unrealistic to encourage you to abandon all thoughts of dating and marriage. I just want to encourage you to avoid making those things your primary focus. Isn't "unfailing love" what you really want? There's only one place to find it. Every date will pale in comparison to the love affair you can have with your Savior.

Make sure you are also pursuing relationships with friends through small group Bible study, campus religious organizations, and daily Bible reading. Wait on the relationship that God has for you, and in the meantime work on making yourself the best you can be for your future mate. You would certainly hope that your future mate was doing the same. Find your comfort in "Unfailing Love." What a great slogan for a T-shirt!

- If you were Natasha, what would your T-shirt say about your dating life right now?

- What expectations do you have for your love life while in college? Are all your expectations realistic? Identify any expectations that need to be modified.

May your unfailing love be my comfort, according to your promise to your servant.
Psalm 119:76 (NIV)

Rubies:

The best boyfriend is going to be a boy who is also a friend. Seek to create and maintain friendships first and see what develops. You can't have too many friends.

Week 6, Day 2

Separating Close Friends

Tracy is an energetic college freshman who works part-time in my office. She usually flashes a big smile and generally seems to be having a lot of fun. I knew she was dating Robert because he comes by the office occasionally, but she rarely mentions him otherwise. Recently, I've noticed a significant change in Tracy. She seems distracted and is obviously troubled in some way. Those big smiles have become rare. Even some of the other work-study students remarked that they didn't think Tracy was in her usual good spirits.

One afternoon, Robert came by the office to visit Tracy. I overheard some heated words as I came into the file room where they were talking. As I entered, Robert brushed past me in a huff. I didn't want to intrude, but I gave Tracy an opening to tell me what was going on if she needed help.

Tracy asked if we could talk. She told me the relationship was quickly declining. Tracy explained, "He never wants me to see my girlfriends anymore. Every time I make plans with them he gets mad or follows us to ruin our good time! I really like Robert, but I've known some of my girlfriends for years, and I need to have time with them, too. I don't understand Robert's attitude."

Tracy is in a situation experienced by many college women. Sometimes boyfriends become overly possessive. At first, the problems are small and his attention might even seem flattering. The guy might say, "I just have so little free time, and I want to spend it with you." However, if these demands accelerate, they may not seem so flattering. A supportive boyfriend will trust his girlfriend to make good decisions about her friends and give her the freedom to spend time with them.

If you ever find yourself in a situation like Tracy's, remember that a dating relationship should not mean that you exclude other friends. You should not feel threatened or stressed because of possessive demands by a boyfriend.

Troublemakers start fights; gossips break up friendships. Proverbs 16:28 (MSG)

Tracy's boyfriend, Robert, is what Solomon would call a "troublemaker," stirring up dissension and separating friends. Many college women make the mistake of neglecting their close female friends to spend time with a boyfriend. Then if that relationship fails, they deeply regret the damage done to other friendships. My closest friendships are with women I knew in high school and college. These precious relationships are definitely worth more than that college boyfriend, whose name has escaped me at this moment.

I hope you are not involved in a relationship like Tracy's. If you are dating, remember that a godly relationship involves mutual respect, trust, selflessness and honesty. Look for a young man who values your opinions, celebrates your successes and is secure enough in your relationship for you to maintain other friendships.

- Have you ever been in a situation like Tracy's? Have you known someone who has? Write some of your concerns here:

- List some of the qualities you would want in a boyfriend. Think of at least 10 qualities you must have in a relationship partner:

Rubies:

Most colleges have a resource center for women who have experienced relationship issues. Find out where your women's center is located on your campus and make note of it. You may need it for yourself or a friend in the future.

Troublemakers start fights; gossips break up friendships. Proverbs 16:28 (MSG)

Week 6, Day 3

Fine Linen and Purple

At least half of the students I counsel in my office are women. The Dean of my business school says he can remember when very few of our students were women. Now they make up not only about half of the population of our school, but they continually garner the most academic awards and honors. These women have shown that they can compete with the guys both in school and in the marketplace after graduation. So why do they try so hard to get attention with the way they dress?

I'm going to try really hard not to sound like someone's grandmother when I say that I am continually shocked at what I see college women wearing on campus. (I guess that probably did sound like someone's grandmother). I like fashion and think it's fun to keep up with the latest trends, but it seems the latest trend of "less is more" has really gone overboard. College women walk around campus wearing less fabric than what I sleep in every night. I hope I haven't lost all credibility here – just hear me out.

The Proverbs 31 Woman has been the standard for Christian women since biblical times. She's the woman we all want to be, the woman every man wants to marry and the woman all of us would want as a mother. Her children and her husband praise her for her diligence and ingenuity. This is not a woman who wants to call attention to her body but rather wants to be admired for her hard work.

She makes coverings for herself; her clothing is fine linen and purple.
Proverbs 31:22(NASB)

College women need to make it a priority to take more seriously the struggle that young men have with the lust of the flesh. This issue is a very real problem for most men. Christians are called to a life of purity, and many women may not realize that their outward appearance portrays more than their grasp of current fashion trends. We tell people every day where we stand on issues of morality without even opening our mouths. There is little reason for a man to believe that you are committed to a high standard of modesty and purity if you're wearing an outfit that tells him otherwise.

It may take more effort, but it is possible to wear the latest fashion trends (at least most of them), and still remain modest in your appearance. Go shopping with friends who are also committed to remaining modest in their clothing choices, and help each other make good purchasing decisions. Having the support of fashionable friends makes shopping more fun anyway.

I imagine the fine linen and purple garments of the Proverbs 31 Woman were the epitome of modesty and sophistication. She was probably one of the best dressed women in town! Aspire to that standard and be responsible with your appearance.

- What do you think about this issue? Do you agree that young women should be more responsible in their dress?

She makes coverings for herself; her clothing is fine linen and purple. Proverbs 31:22 (NASB)

- How do you think our appearance reflects who we are to others?

Rubies:

Remember that first impressions only happen once and your appearance can be very important. Dress conservatively when interviewing for clubs and organizations or even when meeting with a professor.

Week 6, Day 4

The Temple

Ask any student to list their top five college-life struggles, and, if they are being totally truthful, sex will make the list every time. You are constantly bombarded with the message that sex is free, fun and uncomplicated. If it's so fun and uncomplicated, why do so many struggle with this aspect of their lives? Christians and non-believers alike need the answers to questions concerning sexual activity in their relationships, including "how far is too far" when it comes to being affectionate with a boyfriend.

Everybody's doing it, right? I'm sure it must seem that way to you. The latest Department of Health and Human Services report reveals that more than 30% of 18-19 year olds have never had sex. It really is true that NOT everybody is doing it. There are many college students who have not only abstained from having sex up to now, but intend to abstain until marriage.

As a Christian, making responsible decisions about sex is very important for your spiritual life and growth. Christian students always want to know "how far" they are allowed to go physically with their boyfriend and still remain within the boundaries of sinless-ness. It would be great, I guess, if there were some sort of measuring tape that revealed which activities were acceptable and which were not. Unfortunately, there is no such thing. God gives us direction in his Word, but leaves out a lot about the specifics. Read the following verses from 1 Corinthians 6:18-20 (NIV):

Flee from sexual immorality. All other sins a man commits are outside his body, but he who sins sexually sins against his own body. Do you not know that your body is a temple of the Holy Spirit, who is in you, whom you have received from God? You are not your own; you were bought at a price. Therefore honor God with your body.

What does Paul mean when he writes that your body is a temple of the Holy Spirit? He wants you to understand that your physical body is the home, the very residence, of God. We think of church buildings or sanctuaries as houses of God, but He doesn't live in buildings made of brick. He lives in you, in your body. That's why Paul admonished his readers that sexual sins were committed against one's own body. These sins are committed literally against the home of God.

There are no easy answers to the questions you have about sex and dating. Make a prayerful decision about this issue before it comes up when you're on a date or with your boyfriend. Deciding ahead of time how you will handle yourself at the end of a date gives you the confidence to follow through with your choices when the time comes. Discuss your opinions and beliefs openly with the person you are dating. boyfriend who doesn't agree with you on this issue is not someone you want to develop a meaningful relationship with.

Most importantly, remember that your body is the temple of God. Keeping this perspective will help in so many of the decisions you'll make with your dates and boyfriends. God's house should be kept pure, approached with reverence and cared for. Honor God with your body.

- What is your personal decision concerning sex before marriage?

- Regardless of what you have done in the past, prayerfully consider abstinence. Write your thoughts about your choice here:

Rubies:

When it comes to physical intimacy of any kind, waiting is rarely the wrong answer. If you are undecided or feel conflicted about something - wait! Once you move forward, it's very difficult to go back.

Flee from sexual immorality. All other sins a man commits are outside his body, but he who sins sexually sins against his own body. Do you not know that your body is a temple of the Holy Spirit, who is in you, whom you have received from God? You are not your own; you were bought at a price. Therefore honor God with your body. 1 Corinthians 6:18-20 (NIV)

Week 6, Day 5

Love Is...

"If you loved me you would..." How many women, young and not-so-young, have heard this tired, worn-out line? It's amazing that men still use it and even more amazing that women still let it work. When you care about someone, you want them to feel love from you. So it's tough when the person you love asks you to prove it with an action you're either not ready for or don't agree with. In reality, someone who loves you wouldn't dream of using this line.

Read through the classic Love Chapter, 1 Corinthians 13. In this chapter, God outlines the characteristics of true love. Some of these descriptions you've heard many times; love is patient, love is kind. Have you taken any specific notice of the characteristic listed in the middle of verse five? It says love is not self-seeking. The Message paraphrases verse five this way:

Love... doesn't force itself on others, Isn't always "me first," Doesn't fly off the handle, Doesn't keep score of the sins of others.

A self-seeking person uses the love you have for him to get what he wants, hoping you'll buy into the myth that love includes making a personal compromise. For example, Amy has been dating Greg for the past six months. They were both committed to abstaining from sex until marriage. But lately, Greg has been pushing

Amy to go farther physically. Now Amy hears the classic line, "If you loved me you would..." more and more often. She feels that she really does love Greg, and has invested a significant amount of time in the relationship. However, if Greg truly loved Amy, he would respect her commitment through supporting her instead of trying to convince her to change her mind.

Self-seeking people aren't limited to boyfriends and it's not always about sex. In college you'll be pressured to compromise on many of your beliefs and commitments. Your best friend since kindergarten might want you to help her cheat in a class you're taking together. You love her, right? She's struggling with this class, promises to get her act together after just this one test and says, "If you were really my best friend you would..."

Some of the friends you've made in your residence hall are really into partying. They're all too young to drink, but it seems an endless supply of alcohol is available when you're around them. They're nice people and you like their company when they're not completely wasted. And, of course, as a Christian you're trying not to be too judgmental so that you can still be some kind of influence in their lives. Eventually, you'll hear, "If you were really cool you would..."

The best thing to do in these situations is to listen to your conscience. The Holy Spirit has been sent to you to be that still, small voice telling you when a situation isn't right. A person who loves you, a person who is your best friend, or a person who really thinks you're cool won't ask you to make the choice between them and something that compromises your beliefs. Just tell them to save that old, worn-out line for the next girl because you know what love is.

- What do you think love is? Write your thoughts here:

- Have you experienced a situation with a boyfriend or friend who pressured you into doing something you didn't want to do?

- How will you handle a similar situation if/when is arises again?

Love…doesn't force itself on others, isn't always "me first," doesn't fly off the handle, Does n't keep score of the sins of others.
1 Corinthians 13:5 (MSG)

Rubies:

Be cautious about a lot of attention or flattery too quickly from a suitor. Love at first sight sounds romantic, but a person who decides you're "the one" on the first date might be a little insincere.

My Notes:

Seventh Week

Choosing a Major

Diamonds are only chunks of coal,
That stuck to their jobs, you see.
- Minnie Richard Smith

Week 7, Day 1

Be Anxious For Nothing

Dana dragged into my office, dropped her backpack next to my desk and slumped down in a chair. She looked like she hadn't slept in days. It was obvious I needed to put on the full armor of counseling, so after donning the breastplate of compassion and the helmet of reason, I started by asking, "What's going on?" The stress reflected on Dana's face was agonizing as she said, "Lori, what am I going to *do* with the rest of my life?"

I admit to stifling the smallest giggle – not because I didn't take Dana's dilemma seriously, but because I remembered it so well. Dana is a freshman in college and she's already worried about the rest of her life. Perhaps you have the same worries even at this early stage in your college career. It seems everyone from your grandparents to the grocery store clerk wants to know what you are going to *do* with your life now that you're in college.

The pressure starts early. As a child, you started talking one day and the next day people began asking, "What do you want to be when you grow up?" Then in the ninth grade you had to take those horrible aptitude tests and had to indicate what your plans were for a college major. Now that you're in college, you're expected to pick a major before you even take your first class. So much pressure.

Do you know what I told Dana? Relax! Don't be so anxious! Many college students put entirely too much pressure on themselves too early. I remember doing the same thing. I didn't know you could sign up for college classes and still be undecided about a major, so I probably chose too quickly and didn't take the time to explore all my options. You may think if you finish your first semester in college without a definite plan for the next twenty years you'll have made a terrible mistake. Not true. Most colleges and universities will require "core" classes that everyone takes the first one to two years, such as English, math, sciences and humanities. There are plenty of relevant courses to take while you are keeping an open mind about a major.

Don't choose a major quickly due to outside pressure. And don't rob yourself of time to explore several options due to self-imposed pressure. God tells us specifically not to be anxious. Do you believe He is in control of your life even while you're in college?

Be anxious for nothing, but in everything by prayer and supplication with thanksgiving let your requests be made known to God.
Philippians 4:6 (NASB)

Tell God how anxious you are in making the right decision about a major and your life's work. Start out by thanking Him for giving you the opportunity to go to college in the first place. He has a very specific plan for your life, and He won't let you miss it.

- Try this experiment with some professionals you know. Make a list of their names, their undergraduate degrees and their current professions. I'll get you started, and I think you'll be surprised at what you find.

1. Lori
Degree: B.S. Fashion Retailing
Career: College Counselor

2.

3.

4.

Be anxious for nothing, but in everything by prayer and supplication with thanksgiving let your requests be made known to God. Philippians 4:6 (NASB)

Rubies:

Many colleges offer "career exploration courses" or workshops on how to choose a major. Take advantage of these great opportunities to learn more about yourself and more about careers that might best fit your talents and your personality.

Week 7, Day 2

A Tale of Two Sisters

My younger sister, Leslie, and I could not have had more different college experiences. We attended the same community college, graduated from the same university and are both enjoying productive careers in our fields of study. But our paths through the college wilderness were varied.

I was a typical first-born, obsessive-compulsive planner, and therefore could not imagine finishing the tenth grade of high school without a specific course of action for my college years. My mom told me about the work of a buyer for a department store. It sounded interesting to me, so I chose fashion retailing as a major. From the time I was still in high school, I wore college blinders. I never considered another major and never took the time to evaluate how my choice matched up with my personality or values. I loved my college classes, and I had fabulous professors. But once I started working in the industry, I was miserable. I eventually went to graduate school and made a much better choice for my professional future.

Leslie is a gifted kindergarten teacher in Hoover, Alabama. She got all the talent between us for working with little children. Leslie changed her major several times during her college career and even took a year off from classes to work full-time and consider her future goals. I remember the change in her outlook when she finally found the major that was right for her. She made the Dean's List and found new motivation for her studies. Her path became straight.

Leslie and I graduated in the same ceremony. She finished her bachelor's degree and I completed my master's. I remember her saying at the time, "You got two degrees by the time I finished my first one!" That was true, but it took me two degrees to find a career I loved, and it only took her one.

The moral of the story of the two sisters is that there is not a "correct" path through your college career. I firmly believe God directed both our paths and led us to our callings. God has already promised to direct your path as well.

I guide you in the way of wisdom and lead
you along straight paths.
Proverbs 4:11 (NIV)

God's paths are straight even if it seems to you like they are crooked. Don't put undue pressure on yourself to maintain a perfect plan for your college years. I wish I had spent much more time exploring my options. Leslie would tell you not to worry about changing your major if you find a better fit for your personality and values.

Your college experience isn't going to look like anyone else's. Try not to be frustrated if you haven't found the perfect major, even if it seems all your friends are already committed to a course of study. Some students find their calling earlier than others. God is designing the years ahead specifically for you. He wants to teach you His ways and to keep you on the narrow path. Pay attention to His leading through prayer and study, and your path will appear straight even in the wilderness.

- How straight are your paths these days? Write a prayer in the space below asking for clarity and discernment concerning your path at this point in the semester.

- Which majors are you considering? Write them here and list some pros and cons for each choice.

I guide you in the way of wisdom and lead you along straight paths. Proverbs 4:11 (NIV)

Rubies:

I don't know the exact statistics, but many students change their major at least once during their college career. Don't worry if you consider a change in the future – get sound advice and move forward.

Week 7, Day 3

A Sterling Reputation

What if I told you that the job you hold down in college could make or break the beginning of your professional career? You'd probably say, "Yeah, right, Lori! I work at the campus book store and I'm studying to be an accountant. What could the two possibly have to do with each other?" I understand your skepticism. My students who have part-time jobs usually don't see the connection either. But let me tell you about Shannon.

Shannon worked with our orientation team last year. Every summer we have hundreds of new students come to campus to register and receive information about the university. Our student workers are vital to this process. Shannon never did seem to think her role in orientation was very important. She was constantly late, never took any initiative to help the new students and soon garnered the reputation of being lazy. All the advisors were frustrated with her, but there wasn't much we could do about it.

Everybody knows that my friend and fellow advisor, Brandy, is married to Stephen, a manager at a popular local restaurant. Stephen often hires college students. His business is a great place for students to work while in school or even after graduation. Shannon came by the office recently and asked Brandy to recommend her to Stephen for a job. Brandy was happy to offer a recommendation, but it probably wasn't the one Shannon would have liked. "She wouldn't work for us, so I can't imagine she'd work for you," were Brandy's exact words to her husband.

Your reputation will always follow you from one job to the next. Every job is an opportunity to make a great impression on professional people who can help you get the next job. Solomon's wisdom is applicable here:

Earn a reputation for living well in God's
eyes and in the eyes of the people.
Proverbs 3:4 (MSG)

A sterling reputation is better than striking
it rich. Proverbs 22:1 (MSG)

Shannon was exceptionally shortsighted in thinking that she could be a slacker on one job and get a great recommendation for another. Professional people are not willing to put their reputations on the line by recommending undeserving students for jobs in the community. However, all of us go out of our way to recommend students who are dependable, enthusiastic and trustworthy. If you establish a reputation as a hard worker in your student or work-study job, I guarantee your employers will make sure other opportunities are open for you.

Don't be shortsighted like Shannon. Your reputation is important. University professors, advisors and student employers have contacts you will want and need for your professional career. Cultivate an impressive reputation and work ethic so you can "strike it rich" after graduation.

- List some people you know who have "sterling reputations."

- What qualities do these people all possess that contribute to the way others see them?

- What steps can you take to make sure that your reputation remains or becomes sterling?

Earn a reputation for living well in God's eyes and in the eyes of the people. Proverbs 3:4 (MSG)

A sterling reputation is better than striking it rich. Proverbs 22:1 (MSG)

Rubies:

One's reputation is built over time through consistency. If you commit to make a change, understand that you won't reap rewards overnight. Stick to it, though, and eventually you'll see the fruit of your labor.

Week 7, Day 4

A Set of Experiences

Sonya is convinced that none of the classes she is taking this semester will benefit her in any way. "Lori, who is going to care if I know the difference between an isosceles triangle and a parabola?" Freshmen probably don't see the connection between many of the classes they are taking and their future professional lives. Actually, there are a few seniors who don't get the connection either.

It's true that your future employer most likely won't ask you to drop and give him 20 calculus problems during an average day at work. But the process of learning calculus is important. Thinking mathematically is a skill that, if developed properly, can serve you in a variety of ways professionally. Similarly, learning to think artistically is a benefit. It's not just about identifying the difference between a Van Gogh and a Michelangelo painting; it's about the experience as a whole. Exposure to calculus and art makes you a well-rounded, informed citizen of the world, and therefore, a more attractive employee.

The Dean of my college, Dr. Barry Mason, nailed it on the head recently while addressing alumni at a college luncheon. He said, "A degree is a set of courses. An education is a set of experiences." I almost stood and applauded! Try not to think of your education as the drudgery of getting through each individual course and checking them off your list of requirements. The collection of your experiences both in class and out of class is adding to your education which will ultimately culminate in making you ready for your professional life.

Your spiritual life is no different. The relationship you have with Christ would be barren and boring if you approached it as a list of requirements to check off as they were completed. I read my Bible today – check. I prayed before I fell asleep – check. I gave 10% of my money to the church – check. What kind of spiritual life is that? Faith is grown through experience with your Savior. And most often faith is grown through tough experiences. God will lead you through various experiences your entire life, not to give you hoops to jump through for no reason, but to build wisdom and understanding.

Consider King Solomon's writings in Ecclesiastes. Solomon wasn't born the wisest man who ever lived. He became wise through his life experiences.

I devoted myself to study and to explore by wisdom all that is done under heaven… I have seen all the things that are done under the sun. Ecclesiastes 1:13a, 14a (NIV)

Make it your goal to fully experience your education. Look for the big picture as you are taking classes. If you simply cannot find the relevance for a particular requirement, respectfully discuss it with your professor or advisor. I think they will be impressed that you are interested in how one class relates to your overall education. And don't worry, I didn't know what a parabola is either. I had to ask one of my students!

- Which classes are the hardest for you to find relevant to your professional goals?

- Make a list of the classes you are taking this semester. Use your imagination and try to think of one thing in each class to might be able to use in a professional career.

I devoted myself to study and to explore by wisdom all that is done under heaven… I have seen all the things that are done under the sun.
Ecclesiastes 1:13a, 14a (NIV)

Rubies:

Interview a professional in your area of interest and ask them about the courses you are taking. They might have some great insight on how your coursework will be relevant in your future professional life.

Week 7, Day 5

Hurry and Scurry

The student who was just in my office has frustrated the stew out of me! Let's call her Julia to protect the privacy of the not-so-innocent. Julia graduated two months ago but made an appointment to see me today. She was all in a dither. Julia told me she wanted to get information about starting a second major in the upcoming semester. It's perfectly fine to take more classes, but I usually ask why a student wants to return to school. Julia said she couldn't find a job and wanted to make herself more marketable. Here's how part of our conversation went:

Me: How long have you been looking for a job?
Julia: Just since graduation.
Me: What services have you used at the Career Center?
Julia: I'm not sure where it's located.
Me: Which employers have received your resume?
Julia: I posted my resume on one of those on-line sites.
Me: Have you responded to any ads in the newspaper?
Julia: No, I didn't think that was a good way to get a job.
Me: Which former employers have you contacted?
Julia: I've never really had a job before.

Uggg! I finally asked Julia if she thought someone was going to call one day out of the blue and offer her a job. I know you are not actively searching for a professional job during your first semester of college, but Julia is a great example of how students fail to plan early enough for the future. Isn't one of the top reasons you're in college to gain successful employment? Of course, it is! Julia failed to realize that preparing for that first job should have started during college, not after she graduated. Now she is in panic mode. Solomon had something to say about that in Proverbs 21:5.

Careful planning puts you ahead in the long run; hurry and scurry puts you further behind. (MSG)

At this point in your college experience, you don't have to know what kind of job you're going to have for the rest of your life or even what major you will choose. What you need to know is that you must take advantage of the resources and opportunities available to you on campus to prepare for your after-college life. Don't be like Julia and wait until after you've graduated to start making yourself "marketable." Find the Career Center on your campus and get familiar with what they have to offer, attend seminars on resume writing, go to employment fairs just to look around and ask questions. It's better to find out now what top employers are looking for while you still have time to acquire those skills. There is a wealth of information out there, but no one is going to bring it to you. You have to go get it.

Use this as an exercise to explore resources on your campus. Answer the following questions about your college:

- Does your college have a Career Center and where is it located?
- Are there any resume writing services on your campus? Do they charge a fee or is the service free to all students?
- Does your college offer any career planning courses for freshmen or sophomores?
- What professional clubs or organizations are currently available in either the major program you have chosen or in programs you are considering? What do they offer to members in the way of career preparation (i.e. speakers, internships, study/tours)?

Careful planning puts you ahead in the long run; hurry and scurry puts you further behind. Proverbs 21:5 (MSG)

Rubies:

One of my favorite pieces of advice for students is "Any job is better than no job!" Find a part-time job or volunteer position on or near campus where you can work a few hours a week. The extra spending money is nice, but the experience and the contacts you'll make could be some of the most important benefits.

My Notes:

Eighth Week

Just Plain Good Advice

Choose my instruction instead of silver,
knowledge rather than choice gold,
for wisdom is more precious than rubies,
And nothing you desire
can compare with her.
- Proverbs 8:11 (NIV)

Week 8, Day 1

Frequent Flyers

There's a catch phrase often used among administrators in higher education: helicopter parents. We jokingly refer to the parents of college students as helicopters because they are always hovering around. In years past, parents have not been quite as involved in the lives of their college students as they are today. For the most part, parent involvement is great, and I can tell that my students sincerely value input from their parents. Problems arise, however, when the parents want to take on the college responsibilities of their students. Choosing classes, keeping up with homework assignments and class attendance is your responsibility, not your parents'. Every advisor has heard of a parent who even wanted to attend classes with their student!

Most of the helicopter parents are hovering around freshman students. This is a unique, and sometimes difficult, transition for both you and your parents. Just a few months ago you were probably living at home with a curfew and doing chores around the house. At that time you were a Colossians 3:20 student: *Children, obey your parents in everything, for this pleases the Lord* (NIV). Now you're practically on your own. You're making the transition to becoming an Exodus 20:12 adult: *Honor your father and mother so that you'll live a long time in the land that God, your God, is giving you* (MSG).

So how do you transition from God's command to obey your parents to honoring them as you become an adult? It's certainly a transition that doesn't happen overnight. If you are having trouble navigating this new part of your relationship, I can assure you that your parents are, too. Maybe some of these suggestions will help:

Stay in touch. Call or email your parents regularly. They just want to know that you're okay, and they want to be involved in your life. You don't have to tell them everything, but let them know how you are doing. Your university probably has information for parents on-line. Tell them about these resources so they can feel involved and reassured.

Listen to their opinions. One way to honor your parents is to respectfully listen to their opinions, even if you choose another decision. It's likely that your parents have already experienced the things you are going through, and they have insight you don't have. If you automatically assume they don't understand, you'll miss out on some wisdom.

Ask for help. Being independent doesn't mean that you have to do it all by yourself. Some first-time students get into big trouble by trying to take on too much responsibility all at one time. Your family is a great resource and you should take advantage of their willingness to help when you need it.

You're not the only one changing. Remember that when you go off to college, your family may go through changes as well. Your parents may redecorate your room or start to travel more. Sometimes this can unnerve a student who has recently left home. Try to be flexible and honor your parents as they make changes of their own.

Your helicopters may be coming in for frequent landings. Hang in there. The flight schedules will become less frequent as the semester goes along!

- What is different about your relationship with your parents now that you have started college?

- How can you honor your father and/or mother even if you don't always "obey" them or follow their recommendations?

Honor your father and mother so that you'll live a long time in the land that God, your God, is giving you.
Exodus 20:12 (MSG)

Rubies:

Parents usually just want to be a part of what's new in your life. Even if you don't want to tell them every detail, tell them about something. Keep them updated on your involvement in a club, for example. They will feel more like they are a part of your experience.

Week 8, Day 2

Take Good Counsel

A student said to me this week, "So, you just talk to people all day?" Well… yeah, sort of. My job as an academic advisor is to be an expert for the university on issues that pertain to college students. In a school as large as mine, that requires a lot of talking. I guess I shouldn't be too insulted by the fact that someone summarized my job as nothing more than a chat fest. I'm sure that's how it looks from the other side of my desk. Plenty of other responsibilities are on my list of job duties, but even if I did just talk all day, I would still be an invaluable resource for students.

Your advisor is someone you need to get to know as soon as possible. This person will be your best resource for navigating the college experience as efficiently as possible. Typically, an advisor is well versed in all aspects of the college or university. Some of the things advisors help students with include course selection, career planning, personal issues, financial aid, university requirements, study-abroad opportunities, internships and what to do if the dog eats your homework.

Advisors have plenty of help for all kinds of situations, but there are some things advisors don't do. Advisors don't make decisions for you. Advisors don't baby-sit, they don't take responsibility for your bad decisions and they don't call with a reminder that it's time for your appointment. Your education is your responsibility and the advisor is there to be a guide and a sounding board. There are several things you can do to get the most out of a relationship with your advisor:

Be prepared. Don't walk into your advisor's office and expect them to tell you what to do next. It's not rocket science. Make yourself aware of the requirements for your degree program by looking them up online or reading the catalog. Maybe even show up with a rough draft of your schedule so you can have an educated discussion about your options.

Speak up. Make your goals and personal plans known to your advisor so he/she can help you plan your academics. The advisor needs to know about your interests, hobbies and extra-curricular activities to be able to best advise you. All these things are important factors in determining your future professional life.

Visit often. You should meet with an advisor at least once a semester. Students who rarely seek out an advisor miss out on new or developing information. An academic curriculum is not static; it changes from time to time, and you need to get the latest updates. You will also experience personal change over your four years at the university, and your advisor can help with those transitions.

Refuse good advice and watch your plans fail; take good counsel and watch them succeed. Proverbs 15:22 (MSG)

This is wonderful advice from Solomon. Good counsel is available, but you must take it. Hopefully, that student who was so impressed with the fact that I talk all day long was also doing a little listening.

- Where is the advising office for your degree program or college? If you don't know, find out ASAP.

- Make a list of questions you have concerning your degree program, your current or future courses, or even personal issues that you need to discuss with an advisor. Take this list with you for your next meeting.

Refuse good advice and watch your plans fail; take good counsel and watch them succeed.
Proverbs 15:22 (MSG)

Rubies:

Create a folder for all paperwork associated with advising. Put in it copies of your degree plan, any notes you make with your advisor about future semesters, and copies of important documents like contracts or minor sheets. It's always best to keep your own documents in case something escapes from your official file.

Week 8, Day 3

It's Not About the Paper

Sharon just voiced the question I suspect crosses the mind of most college students at one time or another. "Lori, what difference does it make to have good grades when all I need is the diploma?" Students who are going to take over the family business, for example, might think grades on a transcript are meaningless. It's great that Sharon is focused on graduating, but she also needs to focus on graduating well. The paper means nothing without the work behind it.

There are plenty of good reasons to get the best grades you can. For one, the competition out there is fierce. You will compete for jobs with college graduates from all over the world. Plenty of those students will take the easy road by making average grades; don't be one of them. When a recruiter looks at your resume, you want her to know that you put forth the extra effort to be an above-average student. That effort implies that you will also be an above-average employee.

Even while you're in college, good grades can make you eligible for honor societies, internships or organizations that could greatly increase your chances for employment. The contacts you make in college may lead to an opportunity to start your career later. It would be unfortunate to miss out on leadership development or professional organization experience just because you were sliding by on mediocre grades. Graduate school might be in your future, too. Average grades won't help you out when you're competing for a seat in law school or professional school.

Probably the best reason to make good grades is because you can. The Army says, "Be All You Can Be." What a great slogan. Why would anyone want to be a C student when they are capable of being an A student? It's your responsibility and privilege to be the best student you can be. For this season, your life's work is to be a college student. Endeavor to do the best work you can in any job you have. Heed this godly advice from Paul:

Servants, do what you're told by your earthly masters. And don't just do the minimum that will get you by. ***Do your best.*** *Work from the heart for your real Master, for God, confident that you'll get paid in full when you come into your inheritance.*
Colossians 3:22 (MSG)

Putting out the minimum effort will garner you the minimum benefit. I know it seems that you are a servant to textbooks and that professors are your masters, but your real master is God. Your work in college reflects your Master because this is where God has called you to be at this time in your life.

It's not about the paper. The diploma itself is just a representation of your hard work and sacrifice. What do you want your diploma to "say" about you? Will it say you barely got by, or that you expended every effort to be the best student you could be? Work hard and be confident that you'll be paid in full when you reap the benefits after graduation. And, Sharon, that's what difference it makes.

- If you got a diploma just for this semester, what would it "say" about you and your work ethic?

- What improvements, if any, could you make for next semester?

- Just out of curiosity… If you wanted to go to graduate school in the college you are currently attending, what grade point average would be required

Rubies:

One way to be the best student you can be is to complete extra assignments even if you are already passing the class or don't need the extra points. Professors are VERY impressed with students who do more than the minimum amount of work and might be more inclined to make recommendations if you need them in the future.

Servants, do what you're told by your earthly masters. And don't just do the minimum that will get you by. ***Do your best****. Work from the heart for your real Master, for God, confident that you'll get paid in full when you come into your inheritance. Colossians 3:22 (MSG)*

Week 8, Day 4

My Teacher

One of the most beautiful pictures in the Bible is found in John 20. Read through this chapter and try to imagine the scene as John records what is arguably the most significant foundation of a Christian's life – Jesus' resurrection and the empty tomb. See if there is anything new that stands out as you read through the familiar narrative.

Mary Magdalene has come to the tomb early in the morning and discovers the stone rolled away and the body of Jesus missing. She runs to tell Peter and John of her discovery. The disciples come quickly to the tomb, find the evidences of Jesus' resurrection and then return to their homes. But Mary stays in the garden weeping. She's not only mourning the death of her Savior, but the death of her dear friend.

Mary thinks she's talking to the gardener when He asks her for whom she is looking. But when Jesus says her name, she recognizes her friend and calls out in astonishment, "Rabboni!" She's amazed at His presence, shocked that He is alive and surely responds without giving any thought to her address. And what her heart cries out at the sight of Jesus is the ancient Hebrew word for Teacher, *Rabboni*. Mary could have called out to Jesus in any number of ways – Friend, Savior, Master, Lord. Why "Teacher"? Is it possible that out of all the things Jesus fulfilled in Mary of Magdalene, one of the most significant roles he played in her life was that of Teacher?

Mary Magdalene called Jesus her Teacher during a time in history when women were not considered worthy to be taught. Her exclamation was recorded for the millions of women who would read this story and revel in the fact that Jesus – their Savior, Redeemer and Lord – was their beloved Teacher, too.

Mary Magdalene lived in a very different place and time. As a woman pursuing higher education, you have so many options for your future that it's often overwhelming to choose a major or career. Did you know that there are more women in college than men? It's true that for several years now the number of women on campus has exceeded the number of men by 1-2%. You are a student during a time in history when the doors are wide open, and the choices for a professional career are more varied than ever.

You have many teachers in your life right now. It's true that few of them will exhibit the same compassion and patience that Jesus showed to his students. That should make it a little easier to remember that there is only one Teacher. You're getting practice being a student of experts who are blessed with great knowledge in academic disciplines. Remember that the Teacher, Jesus, wants you to be a student of the only knowledge that is eternal – Himself.

Behold, God is exalted in His power; Who is a teacher like him? Job 36:22 (NASB)

The question posed in Job is an easy one. There is none.

- What does it mean to you to have Jesus as your Teacher?

- What is Jesus teaching you this week?

Jesus said to her, "Mary!" She turned and said to Him in Hebrew, "Rabboni!" (which means, Teacher). John 20:16 (NASB)

Rubies:

You already know that your teachers are different from Mary's. Your professors are not Jesus, so don't hold them to that standard. They have flaws and weaknesses just like you. Try to learn something from your teachers no matter their style or teaching method.

Week 8, Day 5

Your Guardian Angel

An amazing thing happened to me several years ago. My friend, LeAnn, was serving as a short-term missionary in Guinea, West Africa, and I was fortunate to get to spend three weeks with her there. I could write volumes about the culture, the food, and the people, but I am anxious to tell you about what happened to me in the market one day.

Guineans go to the open-air market every day to purchase the day's food. It's a fabulous, busy place full of wonderful sights and smells. To this day, the scent of pineapples takes my mind straight to the markets in Guinea. LeAnn and I were wandering around a market one day looking at all the fabrics, the fruits and vegetables and enjoying a rare cool morning. I found something interesting and turned to ask LeAnn how much it would cost. She was gone. I had lost track of her in the rows of merchandise. I could not speak a single word of the local languages. LeAnn was my only means of communication in this world. My heart sank into my stomach. In a split second all I could think was that I was lost in this place where I couldn't speak with any of these people and that LeAnn would never find me.

It seemed like a lifetime, but only a few minutes later LeAnn appeared with one of the Guinean market ladies. I was so relieved that I almost started to cry! The market lady had seen the look of panic on my face when I realized LeAnn was not with me. This kind woman knew she couldn't speak my language, so instead of trying to calm me she just ran off to find LeAnn and bring her back to me. What an amazing feeling to find out that while I was almost paralyzed with fear and my mind was racing through one escape plan after another, someone was already on the move to make things right for me.

See, I am sending an angel ahead of you to
guard you along the way and to bring you
to the place I have prepared.
Exodus 23:20 (NIV)

This has long been one of my favorite verses. My guardian angels have come in many varied packages and in Guinea one was a market lady who only spoke the African language of Susu.

I've told this story to my freshmen students many times and encouraged them to find their "Guinean market lady" in college. There are plenty of people who have already experienced exactly what you are going through during your first semester. Find the person who, while you are exploring this new environment and encountering scary situations, will help to guard you along the way. Often that person is an advisor, a residential hall coordinator, a counselor or a Bible study leader. But many times your guardian angel may come from unexpected places, so be on the lookout for him or her.

- Have you been blessed with a guardian angel (or angels!) since you started college this semester? List them here and write a prayer of thanksgiving to God for their help and encouragement:

See, I am sending an angel ahead of you to guard you along the way and to bring you to the place I have prepared. Exodus 23:20 (NIV)

Rubies:

If you haven't found your guardian angel yet, go look for her! Make an effort to get to know an advisor, a counselor or someone in your residential hall. If you're attending a large university where there are many students to serve, those people might require more effort on your part to fine and get to know.

My Notes:

Ninth Week

Play it Safe

Now the melancholy God protect thee,
And the tailor make thy garments of
changeable taffeta, for thy mind is an opal.
- William Shakespeare, The Twelfth Night

Week 9, Day 1

Home Sweet Home

The university environment is one that makes most students feel like they are right at home. Residence halls look more like apartment complexes, dining facilities resemble restaurants, and the grounds are often manicured to look like city parks. All these things work together to give students and parents the feeling that college is not only a place to study but a place to live. My own university, for example, is like a small city. We have a grocery store, a laundromat, clothing stores, restaurants, movies and concerts all in walking distance. Unfortunately, we also have a crime rate similar a small city's, and so do most college campuses.

My campus feels like Mayberry sometimes. I wish it were. I know how easy it is for students to feel safe on campus, because I feel safe on mine. I also know that university officials do everything possible to make campus a safe place for students. But being safe on campus must be a proactive decision you make every day. Follow some basic guidelines to keep yourself safe:

- Always lock your room and your car.
- Keep valuables out of sight, especially in the car – don't advertise them.
- Don't prop open the main door to a residence hall.
- Don't walk alone late at night on campus – seek out an escort service.
- Use well-lit walkways at night on campus.
- Engrave valuables such as computers or

bikes.

- Avoid going to unfamiliar places with people you don't know.
- Ask safety officials for crime statistics on your campus.

Property theft is the biggest problem on most campuses. If you are living with others, make sure you discuss with your roommates how to handle people coming and going from your room or house. The last thing you want is random people having access to your electronics, CDs or jewelry. If you are riding a bike on campus, register it with the police department and engrave all the major sections. Invest in a good bike lock and use it properly.

Driving and parking on campus is always a hot topic at my university. If you have a car on campus, make sure you keep it in good running condition. Have your car serviced regularly to avoid breaking down at night or in an unfamiliar area. (You wouldn't believe how many of my students miss class because they were having "car problems.") Never pick up hitchhikers or pedestrians in your car. If someone is in distress, you can always phone for help. And, of course, avoid driving or riding with anyone who is intoxicated.

All of these suggestions are common sense, right? You know what to do to stay safe, but everyone needs a reminder. I hope you feel right at home in your residence hall or your apartment near campus. Just keep sound judgment and discernment in sight as Solomon admonished in Proverbs 3:21-23 (NIV):

Preserve sound judgment and discernment, do not let them out of your sight... Then you will go on your way in safety, and your foot will not stumble.

- College and university officials are required to provide crime and safety statistics for your campus. Look these up on your college website. Is it easy to find?

- What stands out concerning crime and safety statistics on your campus? Anything listed there that you didn't know?

Preserve sound judgment and discernment, do not let them out of your sight... Then you will go on your way in safety, and your foot will not stumble. Proverbs 3:21-23 (NIV)

Rubies:

If you are in a study or class group with people you don't know, see if there are rooms available at the library to reserve for your group. You can avoid going to an unfamiliar house and it might also be a more convenient place to meet.

Week 9, Day 2

Mockers and Brawlers

Adrienne hit the ground running when she came to the university last year. She immediately got involved in one of our freshman leadership organizations and gained great experience through committee membership and event participation. By the second semester, she became an officer and assumed a position of leadership for many other members of the group. Adrienne's committees were productive and the other members regarded her as a role model.

Things began to change at the first of this year. Adrienne started showing up late for meetings and wasn't as organized as she used to be. She missed deadlines and started to lose her influence over the other members of the group. Adrienne came to my office to discuss the decline of her recent academic performance, and I quickly realized that alcohol abuse was to blame for more than just poor grades.

Adrienne, like a lot of college students, didn't think the amount she was drinking was any big deal. "Everyone I know drinks a little," she said. The problem was that Adrienne wasn't drinking just a little, she was drinking a lot. For many college students, the point of drinking at all is to get drunk, and more students drink to excess than ever before. Adrienne had lost her positive influence over other students, but she was also putting her college education at risk. Your college degree is worth more than a few beers, but some students still take the risk. Solomon would say they were very unwise.

Wine is a mocker and beer a brawler;
whoever is led astray by them is not wise.
Proverbs 20:1 (NIV)

Who wants to hang out with mockers and brawlers? These verses are a warning to those who believe that alcohol can have any positive influence in their lives. Here are some solid truths to consider:

- Alcohol impairs your ability to be in control. Any number of tragedies can occur while under the influence of alcohol including car wrecks, unprotected and unplanned sex and property damage.
- It takes up to three hours to get the alcohol from only two drinks out of your system. Even coffee doesn't help this process.
- If you drink at the same rate as the guys, you'll become more intoxicated on the same amount of alcohol.
- Alcohol can be dangerous when consumed with many kinds of medications. Even over-the-counter sinus medications can result in adverse side effects. Always follow the directions on your prescription.

Adrienne took stock of her situation and curbed her alcohol consumption before she did too much damage. She found that the rewards of prioritizing her education before partying far outweighed any fun she thought she had found in drinking. Solomon would call that wise.

- You are likely not old enough to drink legally. What is your opinion about alcohol consumption for underage students?

Wine is a mocker and beer a brawler; whoever is led astray by them is not wise. Proverbs 20:1 (NIV)

- Have you made any concrete decisions concerning your personal stance on alcohol consumption? Write it out here:

Rubies:

Did you know your brain is not fully developed until you are 25 years old? Alcohol kills brain cells. Hang on to as many of those cells as you can!

Week 9, Day 3

Everything is Permissible

The debate rages on in Bible study groups and in sermons from Maine to California – is it okay for Christians to drink alcohol? My pastor addressed it just this week as part of a sermon on the role of a deacon. As I said yesterday, the Bible does not forbid drinking alcohol. However, it has plenty to say about drunkenness, such as:

Don't drink too much wine and get drunk...
Drunks and gluttons will end up on skid
row, in a stupor and dressed in rags.
Proverbs 23:19 (MSG)

For you, at this stage in your life, the main issue to consider is that you are likely not old enough to legally drink alcohol. However, the "small" matter of breaking the law doesn't seem to deter many college freshmen. The beer and the wine flow freely in never-ending supply.

But there's more to the issue than simply the law, right? Let's try to address the issue from a spiritual standpoint. Maybe you've heard of "Believer's Freedom." This refers to a passage written by Paul to believers in Corinth. Read 1 Corinthians 10:23-33.

Paul wrote this passage to encourage believers who knew they had certain freedoms in Christ, but were arguing over whether it was still okay to indulge in those freedoms. For example, under the old law, they were forbidden from eating certain kinds of meat. Under Christ, those meats were not off limits, but Paul encouraged the believers to abstain if it would cause someone of lesser faith to be confused or stumble.

A similar issue presents itself with regard to alcohol. Some people think a Christian should never drink alcohol; others contend drinking is okay based on Scripture. However, in our society, alcohol destroys more lives than any other substance. It's the cause of an amazing number of tragedies including addiction, death and violence. In Christ's culture, the social mores about drinking were different. And there weren't as many car accidents, although there may have been some camel collisions, I'm not sure.

In our particular society at this particular time, I think the best choice for Christian college students is to abstain from drinking alcohol, but that decision is completely up to you, and I hope you will make it prayerfully. My pastor said it so well: "Let's not compromise our witness in Christ by taking liberties with our freedom in Christ." If you decide it's okay for you to drink (again, if you're of age), consider whether it's worth it in relation to not only the dangers associated with drinking, but also the potential to ruin your witness for someone of lesser faith and understanding. The Believer's Freedom passage starts out with the best advice when contemplating this issue: seek the good of others first.

"Everything is permissible" – but not everything is beneficial. "Everything is permissible" – but not everything is constructive. Nobody should seek his own good, but the good of others. 1Corinthians 10:23-24 (NIV)

- What do you think about this controversial topic? Should Christians abstain or indulge in alcohol consumption?

- In light of the many tragedies associated with alcohol consumption in our society, do you think believers should exercise their "freedom" to consume alcohol even at moderate levels?

Rubies:

Universities typically have lots of information about alcohol consumption and the consequences of abuse. Even if you choose not to drink, educate yourself on what to do in case a friend or roommate gets in trouble with alcohol. Don't blow this information off if you have chosen not to drink. Alcohol consumption is a big issue for college students and you need to be aware of the dangers regardless of your choice.

"Everything is permissible" – but not everything is beneficial. "Everything is permissible" – but not everything is constructive. Nobody should seek his own good, but the good of others. 1Corinthians 10:23-24 (NIV)

Week 9, Day 4

Lay Aside Every Weight

The dreaded "Freshman 15." To hear some girls talk, the rumor that many college students gain 15 pounds in their first semester is scarier than all the papers required for English class. Do all students gain weight during their first year of college? Well… some research does show that college students gain weight in the first year, but on average, the gain is more likely to be in the four to six pound range, not usually 15 pounds.

What leads to this extra baggage? I'm sure you have discovered by now that the average student's diet is heavy in pizza, chips and soft drinks. Your diet at home was probably more balanced. Late night eating also leads to extra calories. Most students don't go to late night study groups armed with snacks of apples and celery sticks. On my campus, you can order a greasy cheeseburger 24-hours a day, and I'm sure other campuses have similar all-night dining.

Along with being free for the first time to choose your classes and your curfew, this might also be the first time you've been completely in charge of your own food choices. At home, someone else might have made sure you had enough fruits and vegetables available for each meal, but at school you can eat whatever you want. Obviously, cinnamon rolls for breakfast sounds better than oatmeal, right? But making poor choices in your diet not only leads to possible weight gain, it might also affect your sleep, stamina or concentration.

Paul liked to compare the Christian life to a race and encouraged his friends in Hebrews 12:1 (NKJV) with these words:

. . . let us lay aside every weight, and the sin
which so easily ensnares us, and let us run
with endurance the race that is set before us.

The race set before you, whether spiritual growth or school work, could be greatly hindered by extra "weight." Paul knew that spiritual growth would be delayed by anything that distracted believers from the example Jesus set on the cross. In the same way, your academic success will be hindered if you are maintaining an unhealthy lifestyle.

What can you do to avoid the Freshman 15? Here are some suggestions:

- Plan to eat regular meals each day – don't eat at random times.
- Keep high sugar snacks and energy drinks to a minimum.
- Keep healthy foods in your refrigerator for easy access.
- Choose water over soft drinks as often as possible.
- Exercise daily and get enough sleep.

Sometimes young women who start college actually lose weight due to the pressure to be thin. Be smart and maintain a healthy attitude toward your weight. Consult a professional at your campus recreation center to determine the best way to achieve or maintain a healthy weight. Being too thin is as unhealthy as being too heavy. The key is moderation. That's why we have veggie pizza!

- How has your diet changed since starting college?

- What changes can you make to stay healthy this semester?

...let us lay aside every weight, and the sin which so easily ensnares us, and let us run with endurance the race that is set before us. Hebrews 12:1 (NKJV)

Rubies:

Consider taking a nutrition or health class as an elective. You'll learn valuable information about food, exercise and how a healthy lifestyle can make you more successful now and later.

Week 9, Day 5

Lead Me

Africa was once called the Dark Continent because so much of its aboriginal landscape was unexplored by Europeans. I found out how dark the Dark Continent can be while visiting a remote village with missionaries several years ago. We arrived in the village during the day while the sun was shining bright. Up to this point I had spent most of my visit in towns that had electricity. The village had no utilities at all. I used candles in my hut so I wasn't aware of how dark it had become outside as night fell.

The village was throwing a party down the dirt path, and I stepped outside the hut with the others to join the fun. The intensity and completeness of the nighttime darkness was something I have never experienced. It's hard to even explain. My eyes actually hurt from the struggle to search out any spectrum of light. I found myself completely paralyzed by my blindness only a few feet from my hut. The voices of my companions trailed a little in front of me and grew faint as they walked away. Speechless, I didn't even call out for them. Someone realized I wasn't in the group and came back for me. The African ladies were giggling a little at my predicament, but some hands grabbed mine and pulled me to step forward.

My steps were hesitant but the guiding hands held fast to mine. It seemed like we walked for half a mile this way; both of my arms stretched out in front of me, head down, seeing absolutely nothing. As we came closer to the burning lights of the party, I could finally see that my guide was a beautiful African woman. She was facing away from me with her hands extended behind her leading me along the way. Once we were inside the circle of light at the party, she turned to me, smiled and then disappeared into the crowd. I hope she saw my thankful expression because we didn't share a language. I'm not sure I ever saw her again, but I have never forgotten her.

You're my cave to hide in, my cliff to climb. Be my safe leader, be my true mountain guide. Free me from hidden traps; I want to hide in you. I've put my life in your hands. You won't drop me, you'll never let me down. Psalm 31:3-5 (MSG)

The life of a college student doesn't shield you from dark places. In fact, you might be experiencing some of your toughest days. Separation from family and friends, unfamiliar places and the pressure to be academically successful might contribute to a feeling of being lost. Many students experience depression for the first time as a freshman.

When you find yourself in so much darkness that you are speechless even to call out, your Lord and Father who understands all things is there to lead you. His arms are stretched out, his hands are grasping yours, and there is light just ahead. It's understandable to be hesitant, but choose to be led even if you can't see the path you're walking. Walk on. The lights are burning at the party and the dancing is just getting started.

- Have you experienced depression or a feeling of "lost-ness" since starting college?
- Write your feelings here as a prayer for God's leading hands:

- What resources are available on your campus for students who need help dealing with depression? Look it up on line and write down the office location here in case you need it for future use.

You're my cave to hide in, my cliff to climb. Be my safe leader, be my true mountain guide. Free me from hidden traps; I want to hide in you. I've put my life in your hands. You won't drop me, you'll never let me down. Psalm 31:3-5 (MSG)

Rubies:

Share your feelings with a friend. Sometimes people are more than willing to help, but don't know what you're going through. Try not to keep it all to yourself.

My Notes:

Tenth Week

Money, Money, Money

There is gold, and an abundance of jewels;
But the lips of knowledge are a more
precious thing.
- Proverbs 20:15 (NASB)

Week 10, Day 1

Counting Pennies

Jackie works on campus in one of the residential halls so I was surprised to see her one evening serving tables at a local restaurant. "Lori," she said, "I'm trying to make every penny count so I can keep my student loans down." A wise decision, indeed, but I hated to see Jackie putting in so many hours at work. For every student on campus who is driving around in a Benz, there are at least two who are really struggling to pay for school. Students should be careful and wise with their money no matter their financial situation. If you are concerned about paying for tuition, there are many good options to consider for financial help.

I encourage every student to complete the Free Application for Federal Student Aid to determine your eligibility (www.fafsa.ed.gov). This application will cover multiple areas of federal financial aid including:

- Grants – financial aid that does not have to be repaid.
- Loans – financial aid from federal, state or private lenders. Subsidized loans are based on financial need and the loaning agent will pay the interest while you are in school. Unsubsidized loans accrue interest while you are in school, but are not based on financial need.
- Work Study – this program allows you to work part-time on campus which can be a convenient way to earn some extra cash.

Scholarships are also offered through your university. Typically, applications are due very early in the year. If you have already missed the deadline for this year, make sure you apply early for next year. Our scholarship coordinator encourages every student to document any financial hardship their family may have on the scholarship application. Examples of financial hardship include a parent's loss of a job or having more than one child in college. The scholarship committee won't know of your financial need unless you tell them, so take any opportunity to explain your circumstances.

Loans are an excellent resource for students who lack the financial means to attend college. Jackie is a great example of someone who is conservative in her approach to loans. She might be eligible for more money than she has taken out, but she knows that those payments are waiting for her after graduation. I made the mistake of using student loan money to buy things unrelated to my education, and I would definitely advise you otherwise. It's tempting to buy things you don't need just because the money is in your account. Subsidize your loans or scholarship money with a part-time job instead of borrowing more money than you need.

Solomon wrote in Proverbs 22:7 (NLT): *Just as the rich rule the poor, so the borrower is servant to the lender.* Careful planning and good advice about money management will allow your loans to work for you to complete your education. Mismanagement can make you a slave to your loans after graduation; a situation many students find discouraging and regrettable. Take Jackie's advice and make every penny count now. You'll have more pennies to count after graduation.

- When is the scholarship application deadline for your college? Look it up and make note of it here. It's usually early in the fall semester, so don't miss it!

- Are there scholarships available for criteria other than grade point average? Consider applying no matter your academic performance.

Just as the rich rule the poor, so the borrower is servant to the lender. Proverbs 22:7 (NLT)

Rubies:

Here's some advice out of my own personal bank of mistakes: Don't use student loan money for anything other than school-related expenses such as tuition, fees, books, food and rent. Find a way to pay for other expenses (clothes, makeup, trips, etc.) through part-time employment. You'll thank me later.

Week 10, Day 2

Stale Pizza

Amy just bought the most expensive pizza in town for a quick snack on this rainy afternoon. She thinks she only paid $12 for it, but ultimately that afternoon snack will cost much more. Why? Amy bought her pizza with a credit card that is already over its limit and has an interest rate twice her shoe size. Long after the delicious aromas of pepperoni and mozzarella cheese have faded, that charge will sit on her credit card collecting interest and fees. Can you imagine being 25 years old and paying for a pizza you bought the first semester in college? That's exactly what happens when you carry a balance on your credit card in addition to annual fees and all that interest.

College students are easy and open targets for credit card companies. Have you been to the student union building lately? The credit card companies are lined up and offering free t-shirts, mugs, sunglasses – anything to get you to fill out their "no obligation" application form. It seems easy and harmless doesn't it? It's not. Many college students who use credit cards unwisely find themselves in serious financial trouble.

Consider Amy's situation. The average unpaid balance on her credit card is $600 per year with a 20% interest rate. The annual fee of $20 is due in addition to a late fee of $25 because she forgot to mail in her last payment. Amy now owes $165 and she hasn't even started paying for her pizza. Many people, not just college students, use credit cards to put off having to come up with the cash immediately. It seems easy to just pull out a card when your checking account is empty. In the long run, you'll pay more for every purchase.

Do college students need credit cards? Not really. Some students and their parents think credit cards are needed for emergency purposes, to establish credit or just for convenience. In reality, you have plenty of time to establish credit, and debit cards are just as convenient. If you feel you need a credit card for emergencies, get ONE card with a very low limit. I recommend finding a card with the lowest interest rate and setting your limit at $500 – that should take care of most "emergency" situations. Go by your university's credit union or local bank. Those institutions have plenty of information about establishing credit with a low limit card or account. The bankers are also experts on how to avoid trouble with your first credit card.

Paul admonished his readers to be responsible citizens when he wrote,

Don't run up debts, except for the huge debt
of love you owe each other.
Romans 13:8 (MSG)

Paul knew the disadvantages of being in debt and wanted to warn his friends. Staying out of debt keeps you free from making monthly payments. Living debt-free will also help your credit rating when you are ready for the more significant purchases you'll make in the future. Do your research and be cautious about credit cards. Paying off your pizza over seven years can lead to indigestion.

- Which credit cards are you currently using while at college? List your credit cards here and check out the fees associated with each card:

Credit card	Interest rate	Annual fee

Don't run up debts, except for the huge debt of love you owe each other.
Romans 13:8 (MSG)

- What changes can you make to reduce the amount of fees and interest rates associated with your cards?

Rubies:

Another great resource is your campus Student Financial Aid office. Contact that office for detailed information about college students and credit cards. Those professionals have a "wealth" of information to help you reduce your debt or avoid it in the first place.

Week 10, Day 3

Prosperity and Success

Bridget and I were talking near the front desk in my office, and I was getting an ear-full about the brand new sports car she got for her birthday. It has all the bells and whistles a girl could want and probably costs more than my house. After Bridget left, one of our student workers said, "Wow! She sure does have it made!" The envious tone was hard to miss. I had counseled Bridget numerous times and knew she certainly did not have it made. Bridget has had a tough year with family issues no one would envy, but the student worker only heard about the new sports car.

In our society, money is equated with success. Many people believe their financial status is directly related to their success as a person or a citizen in the community. College students are no different, equating financial gain with the epitome of success in life. They are constantly bombarded with a message that says the more "stuff" you have, the more successful you have become. There is absolutely nothing wrong with financial gain, but you want to be successful in the eyes of the Father, not the world.

Even on a college campus, the trappings of success are evident. Students who have only part-time jobs are driving expensive cars and spending large amounts of money on shopping or going out. These students are enjoying the support of their parents and are developing an expectation of financial success that may not be a reality for them personally, especially right out of college. Students who struggle financially through college can get very distracted by the obvious wealth of others and begin to get discouraged by their own situation.

Is God interested in your success? Absolutely! After Moses' death, God gave detailed instructions to Joshua as he prepared to lead the people across the Jordan River and into the Promised Land. God vowed to protect the people and gave Joshua directions concerning success and prosperity.

Do not let this Book of the Law depart from your mouth; meditate on it day and night, so that you may be careful to do everything written in it. Then you will be prosperous and successful. Joshua 1:8 (NIV)

God was interested in the prosperity of His chosen people, and he's interested in yours as well. But it's not always God's will for you to be successful according to the standards of the world. The difference between God's standards and the world's is vast, but Satan finds creative ways to confuse the issue, distorting the truth about success and prosperity in a believer's life.

According to this verse in Joshua, the roadmap to success is found in the Word of God. Learning and meditating on God's Word allows you to build up knowledge and understanding of biblical precepts in your heart. Then you will be able to discern for yourself the difference between worldly success and godly success.

- What are your thoughts on success and financial gain at this time? How do you define success in your future?

- Are your goals in line with what God's Word says about success? Ask God to make you aware of any changes you need to make in a prayer below:

Rubies:

Getting to know people from different backgrounds can give you great perspective on your current financial situation. Volunteer at a community service center or help out with international students on your campus to expand your experience.

Do not let this Book of the Law depart from your mouth; meditate on it day and night, so that you may be careful to do everything written in it. Then you will be prosperous and successful. Joshua 1:8 (NIV)

Week 10, Day 4

Blessing Others

If you were wealthy it would be so much easier to be generous with your money, right? Surely, if you weren't a poor college student, struggling to get by with a part-time job and student loans, it would be a cinch to tithe and give generously to others. Sorry to burst your money bubble, but it's usually just the opposite. The more money you have, the more money you think you need and the harder it is to part with.

I had the least amount of stress in my own discipline of tithing when I was just out of college. My paycheck was woefully small, but I had fewer bills than I do now. It was a joy to contribute to my Sunday School class without worrying about paying the phone bill. Then my student loans became due for repayment, eventually I picked up a credit card bill or two and now I'm a home owner. It definitely takes more commitment and concentration to be generous with my money now than it did then, and I make a lot more money now.

I don't know if there is scientific data on this or not, but my own experience has taught me that people with the fewest number of resources are often the most generous. While traveling to some of the most financially depressed regions of the world, I've found the generosity of the people to be amazing. In Africa, I visited the home of one woman who wanted so desperately to show her gratitude for my visit that she gave me the only fruit she had in her home. I had enough money to buy her fruit for a month, but she gave me all she had and was delighted to do so. The

Brazilian kids I worked with in Rio gave me so many gifts I could hardly find a place to pack them. In Venezuela, I complimented a girl on her earrings just to start a conversation and she took them out and gave them to me. Those are humbling experiences.

Now is the time in your life to develop the discipline of being generous with your money and resources. Don't tell yourself that tithing and sharing your money with others will come with a professional job and a real paycheck. There are many benefits to generosity according to Proverbs 11:24-25 (MSG):

> *The world of the generous gets larger and larger; the world of the stingy gets smaller and smaller. The one who blesses others is abundantly blessed; those who help others are helped.*

What a concept: bless others to be blessed, help others to receive help, give to get even more back. The world tells us that giving generously to receive abundantly doesn't work. But God makes us this promise so we can take it to the bank. No pun intended.

Find ways to fit generosity into your life now while your resources are small. Tithe from your part-time job's paycheck, offer to buy lunch for a friend who is struggling with her budget or pick up some magazines for your roommate when she's home with a cold. These things require only a small amount of money, but the blessings are big. Give generously and watch your world get larger and larger.

- In what ways can you be generous with your money or resources right now?

- Write out your commitment to tithing here:

The world of the generous gets larger and larger; the world of the stingy gets smaller and smaller. The one who blesses others is abundantly blessed; those who help others are helped. Proverbs 11:24-25 (MSG)

Rubies:

One way to be generous on a small income is to donate clothes, shoes, towels, linens and utensils to a local mission or rescue service. Don't keep things you don't use when someone else may be in need.

Week 10, Day 5

Ransomed

Les Misérables is the best Broadway play ever in the history of theatre… in my humble opinion. The story is incredible to the very last scene, but the most amazing part is the beginning. Jean Valjean (pronounced with a French accent, of course) is a criminal recently paroled from prison for stealing bread to feed his starving family. He has no place to stay, but a kindly priest and his wife take Jean in, feed him and provide him lodging.

During the night, Jean, who is mad at God for being unjust, steals the priest's silver serving pieces and runs. The police catch him the next day and Jean swears that the priest gave him the silver. Jean is taken back to the priest to confess, and the most incredible exchange happens.

Upon seeing Jean in the hands of the police, the priest says, "Ah, Jean Valjean, there you are and thank you for finding him, officers. Yes, I did give him the silver, and Valjean, you forgot the candlesticks that are worth at least 2000 franks. Why did you leave them?" The police unhand Valjean and leave. Jean asks the priest, "Why are you doing this?"

The priest grasps Jean by the shoulders and looks intently into his eyes. "Jean Valjean, my brother, you no longer belong to evil. With this silver, I've bought your soul. I've ransomed you from fear and hatred. Now I give you back to God." Jean Valjean goes on to do great things. His life is not free from trials, but Jean is not only freed from his criminal past, he helps many other suffering people as well.

Isn't this the very picture of what God has done for us through His Son, Jesus? As an unbeliever you were just like Jean Valjean; a common criminal looking for nourishment to satisfy your hunger and a place to lay your head. God gave as a sacrifice something much more precious than silver serving pieces or silver candlesticks. With His very own Son, He has ransomed you from fear and hatred, from sin and destruction. With the sacrificial blood of Jesus, your soul has been purchased at a very high price.

"...the Son of Man did not come to be served, but to serve, and to give His life as a ransom for many." Matthew 20:28 (NIV)

The priest bestows great charity toward Jean Valjean, and as a result, Jean becomes a compassionate and merciful friend toward others. Through this one act of love, Jean's life is transformed from evil to good.

How can you show Christ's love to your fellow students? You don't have to spend lots of money. Just use the resources you already have. I'm sure you can see that many of your fellow students are desperate for a kind word or gesture. Be the one in your Bible study, Christian student organization or even in class who reaches out to the students who need a friend. You need not sacrifice silver candlesticks to show mercy and compassion toward a fellow student, just a little of your time and compassion.

- List some people you've met this semester who need a kind word or gesture:

- Who has been kind to you this semester? Make sure they know you are grateful.

"...the Son of Man did not come to be served, but to serve, and to give His life as a ransom for many." Matthew 20:28 (NIV)

Rubies:

Determine to look for ways to be kind or merciful tomorrow. Spend the day actively seeking these opportunities. You'll be amazed how many opportunities come your way and how blessed you'll be for recognizing them.

My Notes:

Eleventh Week

Comfort and Encouragement

The pebble in the brook secretly thinks
itself a precious stone.
- Japanese Proverb

Week 11, Day 1

Shallow Roots

The weeks before Carrie left home for college were a blast. She and her friends had finished a busy senior year of high school and were looking forward to starting their new college lives. All through the summer Carrie shopped for new "college clothes," enjoyed lots of time with her family and hung out with her friends. Carrie had grown up in a small town with her closest girlfriends, so many of them were just like family. They had all talked excitedly about going to college throughout their senior year of high school. This tight group of friends took their entrance exams together and helped each other with all the required application and scholarship forms.

Many of Carrie's friends decided to apply at the local community college, but Carrie applied out-of-state because she was particularly interested in a large university with a good reputation in her major of choice. None of these friends had any idea how much they depended on each other until they were a few hundred miles away at separate colleges.

Carrie and I chatted in my office the other day. She said, "I love being away at college, but here I just don't have any... roots!" Carrie has enjoyed being surrounded by supportive friends and family her whole life, but now she's faced with developing a brand new set of friends. If you are attending college with several close friends, be thankful. But more than likely you're experiencing exactly what Carrie described.

Carrie's dilemma reminded me of two things – a

recent adventure and a great passage of Scripture. Last year I had the good fortune to visit a friend in California. We set out on an adventure to walk through a forest of Sequoia Redwood trees. I had seen pictures of these massive trees but had never seen one in person. Wow! Standing under trees over 250 feet tall is impressive – and a little dizzying. I remember learning in school how deep a tree's root system could grow and visualized the roots from these trees stretching all the way to China! "Nope!" the park ranger said. "The Sequoia's roots are very shallow. They spread out over 100 feet from the base of the tree, intertwining with the roots of other trees, but they never grow down deep. That's what makes them so secure. They support each other."

Embrace this opportunity to make new friends and create a new support system. There is nothing quite as comforting as an old friend – those roots are deep. But new friends can be just as important in surviving your first semester in college. Remember, Jesus is your ultimate support system. He's made a promise to you, and you can count on it.

But blessed is the man who trusts in the LORD, whose confidence is in him. He will be like a tree planted by the water that sends out its roots by the stream. It does not fear when heat comes; its leaves are always green. It has no worries in a year of drought and never fails to bear fruit.
Jeremiah 17:7-8 (NIV)

- Have you made some new friends this semester? Write some of your thoughts on leaving home and making new friends. Has it been difficult? Easy?

- What can you do to make more friends and to be a support for them?

Rubies:

The friend I mention in this story is one of my closest confidantes. We've been friends since high school, but now she lives in California. We keep in touch via e-mail and cell phones. Keeping in touch with old friends is important. Make the effort.

But blessed is the man who trusts in the LORD, whose confidence is in him. He will be like a tree planted by the water that sends out its roots by the stream. It does not fear when heat comes; its leaves are always green. It has no worries in a year of drought and never fails to bear fruit. Jeremiah 17:7-8 (NIV)

Week 11, Day 2

My Psalm 23

Several years ago, during a particularly hard semester in graduate school, I had the opportunity to write my own version of Psalm 23 for a Bible study assignment. I was supposed to choose a role God played in my life and paraphrase the Psalm around the characteristics of that role. I was studying to be a counselor and was probably in need of one at the time! The Lord has certainly been my Counselor over the years, and it was fun to try to define what that means to me in this paraphrase. I want to share it here in case you can relate:

The Lord is my Counselor,
I shall not worry.
He leads me to His word for direction,
He surrounds me with friends for support,
He calms my fears.
He gives me discernment to make good choices
So He can be glorified.
Even though the world offers bad advice
And shallow comfort,
I will not fear separation from God.
Your love and power will shield me.
You prepare a safe place for me away from my
enemies;

You fill my mind with happy thoughts;
My gratitude overflows!
Surely peace and serenity will fill all the days of my life,
And I will rest in the arms of my Savior forever.
-Lori Barstow (White), 1996

I was so thankful for these words. The prose was easy to write, and that's how I know it came directly from God. I am definitely not a poet. I printed these verses on pretty paper and attached it to a bulletin board in my office. Every so often someone will notice and comment. Since writing this piece, I have often thought about all the different roles God has played in my life – father, friend, savior, role-model and companion.

What role is God playing in your life right now? God can play several roles in your life all at one time. If you are lonely, He may be your Friend. If you are discouraged, He might be your Encourager or Comforter. There will be times during this semester when you need God to be your Great Physician or your Protector. Of course, He's always your Redeemer and Father. What a wonderful gift to know that your Savior can fulfill your every need moment to moment.

In the journaling section for today you'll get the chance to write your own Psalm 23. Think about these familiar scriptures in a new and different way. Then post your version on your bathroom mirror, on a bulletin board or in your car to remind yourself daily about who Jesus is to you at this time in your life.

- Write your own version of Psalm 23 in the space below. Who is the LORD to you – Savior, Father, Friend, Master?

The LORD is my shepherd; I shall not be in want.
Psalm 23:1 (NIV)

Rubies:

Try paraphrasing other pieces of scripture that are meaningful to you. Creative writing stretches your brain power which is always good for studying.

Week 11, Day 3

Cast Away

There's a small fishing pond on my grandfather's homestead land in Arkansas. The property is still owned by some extended family members so my cousin, Chad, and I make it a point to get out there with poles and fishing gear as often as possible. We can drive up to a fence on the property, but then we have to get out and walk. By the time we get to the pond, we're completely surrounded by trees, and it's easy to imagine that civilization is miles away.

Chad is not only a skilled fisherman but also a gentleman. He drives the truck, carries the tackle box and baits all my hooks. What more could a girl ask? One of our more hysterical fishing moments happened during a spring break visit. Chad said, "Just don't get your line hung up in a tree." Well, I'm sure you can guess what happened on my next cast. All I reeled in was tree branch.

It looks easy when someone like Chad does it, but casting a line from a fishing pole takes skill. Even after several fishing jaunts with Chad, I'm still in the novice stage of my training. It takes just the right pole, with just the right flick of the wrist, in just the right direction. Most of the time I get all tensed up and sling the hook in a wild pattern, or I forget to take my finger off the line only to find out my hook didn't go anywhere.

Many of Jesus' disciples were fishermen, and I'm guessing they were much better at casting their lines than I am. I'm sure Peter knew what he was talking about when he wrote, *Cast all your anxiety on Him because He cares for you.* I Peter 5:7 (NIV)

For most students, anxiety tends to build over the semester. The end of the semester is much more stressful than the beginning. Some of that anxiety can be alleviated with careful planning and attention to detail early in the semester. But even planning ahead won't relieve everyday stresses that are just part of life. For that kind of anxiety, practice casting your cares on Jesus.

Casting from a fisherman's perspective is physical, quick and takes lots of practice (don't I know it!). Casting your anxiety on Jesus from the spiritual perspective is similar. It takes a lot of effort for us to learn to let go of our anxieties. We want to keep them close, worry over every little thing and act like we're actually in control. It takes practice to cast our anxiety on Him. We might succeed one time, but the next time our anxiety builds up, we're trying to hold on to it again.

The best part of fishing comes after the hook and sinker are in the water. Once all the tension involved in making a good cast is over and the hook is in the water, all I have to do is sit back in the grass, enjoy the weather and wait on the action to start. Cast your cares on Jesus and sit back in the grass. The weather is great!

- What cares can you cast on Jesus this week?

- How can you practice better casting in the spiritual sense?

Cast all your anxiety on Him because He cares for you. I Peter 5:7 (NIV)

Rubies:

Anxiety can take a physical toll on your body making it more difficult to concentrate and fight off illness. Don't take it lightly. If your anxiety has become too much to handle, see your advisor about ways to lighten your load.

Week 11, Day 4

A Little Encouragement

My mom definitely has the gift of encouragement, especially when it comes to her daughters. I got an e-mail from her this week that said "Yea, Lori!" It made us both laugh because of a story we tell often in our family. Years ago, my parents were driving me to a kindergarten program in which I was scheduled to recite a poem. Mom was going on in the car about how proud she was of me and how I would do such a great job. At some point I stopped her and said, "Now listen, Mom, when I do my part, don't stand up and say, 'Yea, Lori!' or anything like that!"

What's really telling about the story is that even at five years of age, I had heard that specific encouragement from my Mom enough times to expect it from her. I knew even then that if I did something well, she would be there to say, "Yea, Lori!" What an amazing gift from God.

A little encouragement can make a significant difference in your outlook, change your perspective and make your day a little brighter. When someone takes the time to support you, with words or otherwise, it's a true gift. Everyone needs a little encouragement. As you work toward the end of your first college semester, you may need some encouragement, too. Here are some words of encouragement straight from God for a few things you might experience at this point in the semester:

Are you a little burned out?

> *Are you tired? Worn out? Burned out on religion? Come to me. Get away with me and you'll recover your life. I'll show you how to take a real rest. Matt. 11:28 (MSG)*

Do you wonder what calculus has to do with anything in life?

> *The heart of the discerning acquires knowledge; the ears of the wise seek it out. Proverbs 18:15 (NIV)*

Are you homesick and missing the comfort of home and family?

> *Praise be to the God and Father of our Lord Jesus Christ, the Father of Compassion and the God of all comfort, who comforts us in all our troubles. 2 Corinthians 1:3-4a (NIV)*

Are you worried about all your new responsibilities?

> *Peace I leave with you; My peace I give to you; not as the world gives do I give to you. Do not let your heart be troubled, nor let it be fearful. John 14:27 (NIV)*

Scripture is full of encouraging words written specifically for you from your Father and Savior. When you need a little encouragement, look to some of these verses and take them personally. I'm sure you also know someone who could use a few kind words. Everybody needs to hear, "Yea, Lori!" every once in a while. Well, maybe not "Lori" but you know what I mean.

- In what areas do you need the most encouragement right now? Write a note to God asking for His comfort – be specific.

- How can you encourage someone else today? Do you have friends or roommates who could use a kind word?

Praise be to the God and Father of our Lord Jesus Christ, the Father of Compassion and the God of all comfort, who comforts us in all our troubles. 2 Corinthians 1:3-4a (NIV)

Rubies:

The smallest gestures of encouragement can mean so much to someone who is stressed out about school or personal issues. Leave a nice note for your roommate, call someone just to say hello or invite a friend to take a study break for coffee or ice cream.

Week 11, Day 5

A Daughter of the King

My friends, Anne Louise, Katy and Ella Grace are absolutely sure that they are princesses. They've been practicing for years. Sometimes Katy might be Snow White, other days Ella Grace might be Cinderella. Anne Louise is old enough now to work for a company that sends out "real live" characters for parties. She was Tinkerbelle last weekend! The younger girls are often adorned in a royal wardrobe and they greet their admiring subjects for photographs. As they grow and revel in this fantasy world, they are also learning about being a daughter of the King. Did you know that you are the King's daughter?

I will be a Father to you, and you will be my sons and daughters, says the Lord Almighty. 2 Corinthians 6:18 (NIV)

Doesn't every little girl long to be a princess? The little princess dresses up in crinolines with sparkling fabric, fixes a plastic tiara over her hair and gives tea parties all day long. Her mom's shoes are too big and the pink lipstick is smeared, but when the princess looks in the mirror she knows that she is absolutely "deee-vine!"

And what's the best part of being a princess? The best part is knowing that as a princess you are the daughter of a King. The King is strong and wise. The princess rests in the King's protection and he makes sure that only good things come her way. The reason the princess gets to dress up and have tea parties is because the King makes it possible.

You may not feel like much of a princess right now. There are so many things on your mind – four tests next week, two papers due, errands to run, people to see and a calendar full of things that can't wait another day. College is demanding, and you haven't noticed a chauffeur in a white carriage waiting outside your residence hall to take you to your next class. When you are completely responsible for yourself and separated from your family, you can definitely get the feeling that no one is looking out for you.

He holds victory in store for the upright, he is a shield to those whose walk is blameless, for he guards the course of the just and protects the way of his faithful ones. Proverbs 2:7-8 (NIV)

The King is already protecting your way. Rest in His protection and revel in the fact that you are a daughter of the King – a real princess! When deadlines are looming and you are stressed out, remember that the King knows how much pressure you are under and He wants to give you peace in the middle of your busy schedule. When you are convinced that not another math formula could fit inside your brain, remember that the King has already provided you with the intellect and ability to accomplish the task.

Every princess knows that her King is standing by waiting for her call in times of need, so don't forget to call on your King. Every princess also knows when it's time to take a break and have a tea party.

- What does it mean to you to be a daughter of the King?

I will be a Father to you, and you will be my sons and daughters, says the Lord Almighty. 2 Corinthians 6:18 (NIV)

Rubies:

During a particularly stressful time of the semester, get your girlfriends together and have a Princess Tea Party. You'll have a "royal" time and make lots of great memories!

My Notes:

Twelfth Week

The Race

There are three things extremely hard:
steel, a diamond, and to know one's self.
- Benjamin Franklin

Week 12, Day 1

The Race Set Before Us

The Christian life is often compared to a race. Paul encouraged believers in their spiritual life by writing, "let us run with endurance the race that is set before us…" in Hebrews 12:1 (NASB). You may feel at this point in the semester that you're running a race called My First Freshman Semester and it's a marathon.

I walked (not to be confused with running) 39.3 miles in a charity marathon a few years ago. The training was difficult and time consuming, but completing the marathon with my friends was so rewarding (even if it was painful). I put many miles on my tennis shoes before the walk, but somewhere around the 20th mile, I still wished I had trained harder. Marathon runners and walkers develop their athletic ability and achieve their goals through stages. We can learn a lot from them and gain both encouragement and inspiration for your college semester. Let's focus on those stages this week.

Preparation is the first step for anyone who wants to participate in a marathon. Can you imagine just waking up one day and going out to run 26 miles? If you had never exercised in your life, this would be an impossible and dangerous feat. Athletes practice hours a day for weeks and months before a marathon, clocking hundreds of miles on the pavement. They also invest in the appropriate equipment, making sure their shoes, socks and clothing are maintained and efficient. Eating healthfully and getting enough sleep is also a priority as the marathon runners attempt to keep their bodies in the best shape possible.

Another fantastic benefit from preparation is that it reduces the frequency and number of unexpected events. Surprises on your birthday are a lot of fun, but surprises in the classroom can be a pain. If a professor calls on you in class, and you haven't read the material, you could be embarrassed, at the least. If you're unprepared for class and you have a pop quiz, you might not only be embarrassed, but your grade could be affected. Marathoners want to be as prepared as possible to avoid any such surprises, and you should, too.

You need to approach each semester the way a marathon runner would approach a race. Prepare ahead of time for success. Here are some suggestions:

- Get the right equipment: textbooks, calculators, pens, notebooks, extra readings. Make sure you have what you need for every class.
- Preparing ahead of time for class means reading ahead in the text and completing all assignments on time or early.
- Study at least a little each day so that you don't have to cram. Review your notes, filling in gaps or clarifying your writing.
- Be healthy. Getting enough sleep and good nutrition will increase your capacity to pay attention in class and soak up all that knowledge.

The "race" set before you is longer than the average marathon so preparation is even more important. Make these suggestions part of your training and prepare for a successful semester.

- Rate yourself on how prepared you were to start this semester:

not at all / somewhat prepared / very prepared!

1---2---3---4---5---6---7---8---9---10

- List some things you could have done to be more prepared for this semester:

Let us run with endurance the race that is set before us...
Hebrews 12:1 (NASB)

- What would you like to do differently to better prepare for the next semester?

Rubies:

It's never too late to prepare. If you didn't prepare well for this semester, begin by preparing well for the next test or the next class. Learn from this semester so that the next one can be even better.

Week 12, Day 2

Developing Perseverance

The preparation phase of the charity marathon I participated in was a comedy of errors for me. My walking partner and I started our training walks by completing five miles and increased our mileage every weekend. The first time I walked 10 miles I tore a ligament in my left foot. It was so painful, but I thought I would have enough time to heal and continue my training before the marathon. A few weeks later, I left for a two-week travel class with my students. On the very first night, I tripped over a suitcase in the hotel room and broke a toe. You guessed it, on my left foot.

I thought about quitting a million times, but so many people had donated money to sponsor me, and I felt awful about bailing out. The marathon stretched out over two days. At the halfway point on the first day, the walkers were given an option of going back to the hotel on a bus. I sat on a curb gazing longingly at that bus. Lots of people were getting on the bus. I could be one of them. No one would blame me because I was so banged up.

Don't you see lots of students bailing out at this point in the semester? They have worked hard for the first few weeks, and then they give up at the halfway point or when the end is just in sight. Maybe they think the work is too hard. More than likely, they just aren't willing to put in the time and effort to persevere.

Perseverance is the second phase of the race for a marathon athlete. That bus pulled away without me the first day of the marathon. I was hurting, tired, sweaty and stinky, but I looked forward to how good it would feel to finish the entire marathon. Perseverance is all about sticking with your plan when the easiest way out would be to quit.

Although it may be easier to put off homework and go out with your friends, stick with your plan to be prepared for the next class instead. Reviewing your notes about chemistry or astronomy might not sound as exciting as reading the latest John Grisham novel, but keep in mind how great it will feel to ace the next test.

James 1:2-4 (NIV) gives us some insight into why perseverance is so important in life, as well as in college:

Consider it pure joy, my brothers [and sisters!], whenever you face trials of many kinds, because you know that the testing of your faith develops perseverance. Perseverance must finish its work so that you may be mature and complete, not lacking in anything.

Successful completion of your first college semester can definitely try your faith, among other things. The trials of this semester will help develop your perseverance so that you "may be mature and complete," a worthy goal.

I can't tell you how proud I am of completing every step of that marathon. I finished last among all my friends who were walking, it took weeks for all my blisters to heal and I still have a few scars. But perseverance provided for me a great accomplishment. Persevere. It's worth it.

- In what areas do you need the most perseverance?

- List some points of inspiration you can use to persevere through this week:

Consider it pure joy, my brothers [and sisters!], whenever you face trials of many kinds, because you know that the testing of your faith develops perseverance. Perseverance must finish its work so that you may be mature and complete, not lacking in anything.
James 1:2-4 (NIV)

Rubies:

Copy James 1:2-6 and post it on your bathroom mirror or on the calendar you use for your academic assignments. Use this Scripture to remind you of the importance of perseverance.

Week 12, Day 3

The Wall

Marathon runners will often talk about hitting "The Wall" during a race. If you know any marathon athletes, you may have heard them talking about working through this very difficult part of the competition. It usually happens around mile number 20. The runner feels like she has lead in her legs, she might lose feeling in her feet and generally feels like her body is carrying twice its weight. Hitting the wall is all about losing energy. At this point in the race, a runner can encounter some serious self-doubt and risk the possibility of quitting.

My students seem to hit the wall about 10 weeks into the semester. Right before the Thanksgiving holiday, it looks like everyone needs a really good night's sleep. The students started out the semester with lots of energy and great intentions, but at this point in the semester many of them have had too much fun, too many late night study sessions and too much junk food.

Marathon runners at the 20th mile and college students in the 10th week of a semester need the same thing: *focus*. Marathon professionals offer many suggestions concerning breaking through the wall. Solomon offered this advice which is applicable to runners and college students:

Let your eyes look straight ahead, fix your gaze directly before you. Make level paths for your feet and take only ways that are firm. Proverbs 4:25-26 (NIV)

Remember that this semester is like a marathon, not a sprint. Keep your focus on your goal of finishing strong. Here are a few suggestions for breaking through the wall of this semester:

- **Get some rest!** If you are overly tired, you can't do your best.
- **Eat your veggies.** Good nutrition will keep your energy up and help you avoid that "Freshman 15."
- **Get in God's Word every day**. Scripture is where you will find your true purpose for the semester and get great encouragement for your struggle.
- **Resort to bribery.** Promise yourself a manicure or a massage if you complete all your assignments for the week.
- **Review your priorities.** Are you spending too much time having fun and not enough time studying? At the end of the semester, you'll be glad you put in a little more work.
- **Keep specific college and career goals in mind for inspiration.** Write down a list of goals for your college career if you haven't already done so.

Breaking through the wall is a great feeling. If you stay focused on your goals and seek encouragement from Scripture, you'll find the rewards to be rich and powerful. You'll gain strength and understanding from the experience for the next time you face a challenging marathon. And that might be as soon as next semester!

- Have you hit The Wall yet this semester? In what ways do you need a break-through?

- List a few goals here that you have for the final weeks of this semester:

Let your eyes look straight ahead, fix your gaze directly before you. Make level paths for your feet and take only ways that are firm. Proverbs 4:25-26 (NIV)

Rubies:

I'm a big fan of small study breaks. Don't try to study for hours at a time. After an hour of concentrated study, take 5 or 10 minutes to grab a healthy snack or walk outside for some fresh air. You'll be able to keep your focus and be more productive.

Week 12, Day 4

Passion and Joy for the Race

The outfits worn by charity marathon walkers are outrageous. Each participant wants to stand out and show their support for not only the cause but people they know affected by a disease or situation. I saw leopard print hats with feather boas wrapped around the brim, neon colors worn by teams of walkers so they could find each other in the crowds and colorful signs with slogans or the names of family and friends. If you were observing from the sidelines, you'd see walkers who were obviously great athletes and some who were barely getting by. But one thing all the walkers have in common was *passion*. These people care about their cause and are excited to be in the marathon.

Passion is as much a requirement for a marathon runner or walker as is preparation, perseverance or focus. A runner without passion will easily tire and find it difficult to stick to her training routine, much less finish the race. As a college student, you also need to find a passion for the marathon of finishing your semester or your degree program. Does this mean you have to do back flips over calculus? Not necessarily, although being enthusiastic about learning anything in college is an asset. But let's be realistic and assume you won't be thrilled with every class.

Finding passion for your studies lies in keeping your ultimate goal in the forefront of your mind. Most likely, you are in college because you want to complete a Bachelor's degree and pursue a successful career.

You are not in college exclusively for any of the individual classes, but for the whole learning experience.

Focusing on the big picture of receiving your diploma and walking across the stage at graduation can help you find passion for your day-to-day coursework. Paul writes that Jesus used this strategy to endure extreme hardships on His way to the cross. He kept the ultimate goal in mind.

> *Let us fix our eyes on Jesus, the author and perfecter of our faith, who for the joy set before him endured the cross, scorning its shame, and sat down at the right hand of the throne of God. Consider him who endured such opposition from sinful men, so that you will not grow weary and lose heart. Hebrews 12:2-3 (NIV)*

Obviously any trials you experience in college can't compare to what Jesus endured, but I want you to focus on how He endured and did not lose heart because of the "joy set before Him." Think about your graduation ceremony. All your friends and family will be gathered for the big event. You'll dress in your cap and gown, and the band will play. When you walk across the stage to receive your diploma, you won't think about all the hardships you've endured to get there. You won't think about how much you had to study or all the late nights of cramming for exams or writing papers. You'll only think about the joy of graduation. Keep the hope of that joy set before you this semester and don't lose heart. The band is already warming up for your ceremony!

- Are you passionate about your college experience? In what areas could you use more passion?

- List again some goals for college. Does keeping these things in mind help to stimulate some joy during the hardships?

Let us fix our eyes on Jesus, the author and perfecter of our faith, who for the joy set before him endured the cross, scorning its shame, and sat down at the right hand of the throne of God. Consider him who endured such opposition from sinful men, so that you will not grow weary and lose heart. Hebrews 12:2-3 (NIV)

Rubies:

Steer clear of people who are not only lacking passion, but are negative about college life. Seek out students who think college life is fun. Their passion might rub off on you and then you can pass it on as well.

Week 12, Day 5

Finish Strong

Walking across the finish line at the marathon was an exhilarating experience. For just a few minutes, all the pain in my legs disappeared and I felt only the praise from the other marathon walkers who had already finished. I had prepared well, persevered through the tough spots and maintained my passion for the event. But the best part was *finishing strong.*

Paul wrote to Timothy about his own race:

This is the only race worth running. I've run hard right to the finish, believed all the way.
2 Timothy 4:7 (MSG)

I love the part where Paul writes that he believed all the way. Remember that Paul's race included imprisonment, physical beatings and many life-threatening situations. In light of those enormous obstacles, he still ran hard right to the finish. A study of Paul's life and trials would lead anyone to believe that Paul had every reason to slow down at the end. Who would blame him? Yet his passion and joy were evident, possibly stronger, to the very end of his life.

Students who have worked hard all semester seem to think they can coast through the last weeks. Many feel as though they have put in all the study hours they can stand. Stephanie was in my office the other day and she said, "I've worked hard all semester, I have A's in all my classes, and for the next two weeks I'm taking a break!" What a huge mistake. Stephanie's A's can turn into B's, or worse, in the final weeks of the semester.

If you have prepared well, persevered through the hardest classes and found a way to be passionate about English Composition (or just college, in general), don't throw it away in the final weeks of the semester. Keep the end goal of a successful first semester in the front of your mind. Here are some tips from students who have finished strong:

- Go to every class toward the end of the semester. The professors give out important information for final tests and projects.
- Assignments handed in at the end of the semester are what the professor might remember when assigning final grades, so make a good impression.
- Pay attention to your health and take care of yourself. The wear and tear from a grueling semester can catch up to you in the way of a cold or fatigue.

As I crossed the finish line of my marathon, one of the event staffers said, "Great job! You did so well!" I thought she would have had a different opinion if she had seen me burst into tears right before the lunch break. But she only saw me finish the marathon and, in her opinion, I must have looked strong. Remember that the end of a semester is just as important as the beginning. Pace yourself, and run in such a way as to finish strong, believing all the way.

- How are you going to finish your race this semester?

- What lessons will you carry over to the next semester?

- What will you do differently?

This is the only race worth running. I've run hard right to the finish, believed all the way. 2 Timothy 4:7 (MSG)

Rubies:

Don't miss the last day of class before your final exam. You could miss out on valuable information about the test that your professor may add or change at the last minute.

My Notes:

Choose my instruction instead of silver,
knowledge rather than choice gold,
for wisdom is more precious than rubies,
and nothing you desire
can compare with her.

Proverbs 8:10-11 (NIV)

Acknowledgments

Many thanks to my mom, Sammie Jo Barstow, for the support, encouragement, wise counsel and editing through both editions of this book. Thank you for passing on a love for books and for our Savior. A godly mother is an indescribable gift and I am one blessed daughter!

Thank you, Ellen C. Maze, for making this book so gorgeous! Ellen, a bestselling novelist and The Author's Mentor, is a blessing to her authors. You can see the evidence of her work in this book, but check her out at www.ellencmaze.com.

Eric White, my very own. You are an amazing husband and father. The gift you are in my life is so far beyond what I deserve, and I am grateful. I love you!

About the Author

Lori White is the Director of Undergraduate Academic Advising for the Culverhouse College of Commerce and Business at The University of Alabama. Her list of job duties is not nearly as long as her job title. Roll Tide!

Lori teaches freshman orientation classes for new college students every fall semester. When she's not meeting with students, she's enjoying the new additions to her family – husband, Eric, and steps, Michael and Mavinee.

Please join the author at Facebook.com / Precious Stones & Alabaster.

49611985R00130

Made in the USA
San Bernardino, CA
30 May 2017